ON THE ROCKS

Amy Rosenthal

ON THE ROCKS

OBERON BOOKS
LONDON

First published in 2008 by Oberon Books Ltd
521 Caledonian Road, London N7 9RH
Tel: 020 7607 3637 / Fax: 020 7607 3629
e-mail: info@oberonbooks.com
www.oberonbooks.com

'Keep the Home Fires Burning'
Words by Lena Guilbert Ford & Music by Ivor Novello
© Asherberg Hopwood & Crew Ltd. All rights administered by
Warner/Chappell Music Ltd, London W6 8BS. Reproduced by
permission.

A catalogue record for this book is available from the British
Library.

ISBN: 978-1-84002-859-1

Cover design by Dan Steward

Printed in Great Britain by CPI Antony Rowe, Chippenham.

Dedicated to the memory of Jack Rosenthal.

A great many people have enabled, encouraged and inspired this play. The author wishes to thank them all, with special mention to: Mel Kenyon; Frances Poet; Anthony Clark; Clare Lizzimore, Ed Stoppard, Tracy-Ann Oberman, Nick Caldecott, Charlotte Emmerson and Paul Burgess; Simon Robson; Josefina Gabrielle; Bruce Hyman; Helen Rix; Jennie and Arthur Hancox; Maureen, Adam and Taina Rosenthal and Phil Porter.

Characters

DAVID HERBERT LAWRENCE

FRIEDA LAWRENCE

KATHERINE MANSFIELD

JOHN (JACK) MIDDLETON MURRY

The action of the play is set in two adjacent cottages on the North coast of Cornwall near the tiny granite village of Zennor. The year is 1916. We can see the tiny front room of Mermaid Cottage, and the larger living/dining room of Tower Cottage, with its open fireplace. Above this is a small turret room. Outside the two cottages is a patch of communal grass and the suggestion of a vegetable patch.

On the Rocks was first performed at the Hampstead Theatre on 26 June 2008, with the following cast:

LAWRENCE, Ed Stoppard

FRIEDA, Tracy-Ann Oberman

KATHERINE, Charlotte Emmerson

JACK, Nick Caldecott

Director Clare Lizzimore

Designer Paul Burgess

Lighting Designer Jon Clark

Sound Designer Edward Lewis

Act One

SCENE ONE

Early morning. DAVID LAWRENCE sits at the table in Mermaid Cottage. The curtains are drawn. He is trying to write a letter, but the pen keeps slipping from his fingers.

LAWRENCE: My dear friends. Dear friends.

>   *He drops the pen.*

>   Damn this.

>   *He picks it up.*

>   My dear friends –

>   *He drops it again.*

>   Hold *still.*

>   *He tries once more.*

>   Dear friends –

>   *It slips again. Frustrated, he grabs it and flings it across the room.*

>   Damn and blast this!

>   *He puts his head in his hands. After a moment, enter FRIEDA, yawning, in a lacy, tattered robe. She finds an apple on the table and takes a huge bite.*

FRIEDA: Mm! Such hunger I have! I dreamed I was at the Saturday market in Metz with my mother and Nusch. Such *good* things to eat we bought, cheesecakes and cream-cakes and macaroons, and on the tram a soldier with a wooden leg was laughing so I took a macaroon and popped it in his mouth and suddenly we all were at the Oper Leipzig. Is that really do you think about sex? Is it raining? Are you working? How dark you always have it!

9

She tears open the curtains. Light floods the room.

Ugh, there he is. Yoo-hoo, Mr Postman! How he hates us! He was preaching in Chapel last Sunday, the farm girls said, and half his sermon was about just me and you. We are quite famous, darling! Which do you think hates us the most, the Chapel preacher or the vicar? I shall make him fall from his bicycle, watch.

She shrugs her robe from her shoulders and exits in a flimsy slip. LAWRENCE goes into the kitchen. The door slams, off, and FRIEDA returns, holding a large envelope. Her sunny mood has evaporated. LAWRENCE appears in the doorway with a pan.

LAWRENCE: Want breakfast?

Beat.

What's the matter?

FRIEDA: From Ernest's sister. It must be photographs, the Easter term. I wrote and asked, remember?

LAWRENCE: Well, aren't you going to open it?

She bursts into tears.

Oh, Christ Almighty. Give it here.

FRIEDA: Don't touch it!

LAWRENCE: Please yourself.

He exits to the kitchen. FRIEDA drops into a chair, clutching the envelope, weeping.

LAWRENCE reappears with a wooden spoon.

(*Brutally.*) Scrambled eggs?

FRIEDA: How can I eat?

LAWRENCE: All right then, don't.

He exits again. FRIEDA shakily opens the envelope. She draws out some photographs.

Clutching them to her chest, she wails silently.

LAWRENCE enters, whistling, with a tray of crockery. He lays the table carefully for one, and exits.

With a great effort, FRIEDA forces herself to look at the pictures, smiling through her tears as she pores over them.

LAWRENCE brings in a loaf of bread, which he puts on the table. He exits. After a while, he returns with a pan of scrambled egg and a pot of tea. He spoons the eggs on to his plate, cuts a slice of bread, sits and eats calmly.

FRIEDA, crying less now, eyes his food enviously. She gets up and goes into the kitchen. She returns with a plate.

She smashes it over his head.

LAWRENCE drops his fork and sways. FRIEDA hops from foot to foot, scared and excited.

FRIEDA: You brought it on yourself!

He touches his head. Stares at the blood on his hand.

You drive me to it, Lorenzo!

Half-rising, he fumbles for a handkerchief and holds it to his brow. Blood seeps through.

How can I forget them? How can you expect it? Four years is nothing, four years goes like that! (*She snaps her fingers.*) *Twelve* years I brought them up, I brushed their hair, I tied their shoes – how should I then stop loving them? I can't! The pain gets only worse!

LAWRENCE: Then don't ask for their wretched photographs, don't dwell and mull and wallow in it. It's disgusting, it's degrading to watch you wallow in your souped-up sentiment. It sickens me. You made your choice, now live with it.

FRIEDA: I *had* no choice! And every day I live with it!

LAWRENCE: Then don't. Go back to your bloody children, I'm sick of it all.

FRIEDA: Oh, I wish I could! I wish I could go back!

LAWRENCE: Go back then! No-one's stopping you!

FRIEDA: Yes, you'd be glad without me, wouldn't you? You'd have just what you wanted all along, a miserable kingdom with yourself alone –

LAWRENCE: That's right!

FRIEDA: A miserable despot of a jumped-up little king with nobody to bully but himself –

LAWRENCE: With nobody to bleed me dry, to suck the living soul out of my body!

FRIEDA: Do you think I want your filthy soul? I don't want any part of you!

LAWRENCE: Sod off then! Cheerio! Goodbye!

Neither moves. A long, exhausted silence. LAWRENCE finally takes the handkerchief from his head.

FRIEDA: Is it bleeding still?

Beat.

Lorenzo, is it bl–

LAWRENCE: Don't think so.

FRIEDA: Does it hurt?

LAWRENCE: Not much.

FRIEDA sits down heavily. She glances at the papers on the table. LAWRENCE moves to cover them.

Don't.

FRIEDA: What is it?

LAWRENCE: Nothing. This wretched palsy. Still can't hold the pen.

FRIEDA: Let me see.

LAWRENCE: No –

FRIEDA: Just the hand, I mean.

He holds out his hand. She studies it.

It will come back, the strength, the doctor said.

LAWRENCE: I didn't trust that Cornish quack.

FRIEDA: Well, tell me what to put, and I can write for you.

LAWRENCE: No –

FRIEDA: Why not? Sometimes we did for *Sons and Lovers.*

LAWRENCE: Leave it. Please.

FRIEDA: But if you are inspired –

LAWRENCE: It's not – it isn't –

FRIEDA: What?

LAWRENCE: It's just a letter, Frieda!

FRIEDA: Oh?

LAWRENCE: To Jack. To Jack and Katherine.

Beat.

FRIEDA: Why? Why do you want them so? What's wrong with being just the two of us?

He stares at her, speechless.

All married people quarrel!

LAWRENCE: Not like this.

FRIEDA: Like what?

LAWRENCE: Like bloody *this*!

He gestures to his head, the bloody handkerchief, the smashed plate.

FRIEDA: Then what would change if they were here? It would be just the same, only with Jack and Katherine watching us as though we are a Punch and Judith show.

LAWRENCE: (*Smiling.*) And *Judy*.

FRIEDA: I *said* Punch and –

LAWRENCE: Only I don't think it would. If they were here, the balance would be different. Everything would change. We'd not be forced into this burning isolation, this hot unnatural intimacy that –

FRIEDA: Lorenzo, this is marriage!

LAWRENCE: *But it doesn't have to be!*

Beat. He leans urgently towards her in his eagerness to be understood.

This is what kills love dead, Frieda. This grim inseparability, as though from the moment we declare our love we ought to be clamped in an eternal embrace. As though because we share our hearts, we share our lungs and liver and bowels as well – we don't! We're separate creatures, why should love make Siamese twins of us? Of course we fight! It's more than any love can stand!

Beat.

Look, why can't we live as a *community,* with other friends, who love us, and who understand? Then we can go apart and be our own free selves with other people – and come back to each other renewed.

FRIEDA: Because we don't have any friends! Because you've brought us to a godforsaken place where no-one likes us!

LAWRENCE: Then let's have Jack and Katherine. They like us. Why not?

Gently:

The cottage next door's empty. I asked Captain Short and he said they might have it cheap if I could fix it up myself. We'd share the kitchen with them, cook and eat with them – and still be alone with each other at night. Wake up in each other's arms and have our friends to spend the day with. You'd have Katherine to tell if I was being mardy; I'd have Jack to talk about my work –

FRIEDA: *We* talk about your work. Always we do. Every book.

LAWRENCE: I know –

FRIEDA: What can he give that I cannot? Oh, I know he's oh-so-clever but –

LAWRENCE: Jack Murry's more than clever. He's a man of the future. And he and I, we kindle each other – spark ideas between us – he makes me think. He makes me want to write.

FRIEDA: Jack Murry makes you write?

LAWRENCE: I swear to God, I'd start again, if he were here.

Beat.

FRIEDA: All right then, quickly, or I change my mind.

LAWRENCE: What –

FRIEDA: Fetch me your pen and tell me what to put.

LAWRENCE: (*Tenderly.*) Frieda –

FRIEDA: (*Looking at the papers.*) Is this all you have? 'Dear friends'?

LAWRENCE: No, no, I have it in my head. Wait…wait.

He paces the room, working out what he wants to say.

'Dear friends. I am very glad that you are happy.'

FRIEDA: *That's* a lie already!

LAWRENCE: No it isn't. 'That is the right way to be, a core of love –' – no, not a core, 'a *nucleus* of love between a man and a woman, and let the world look after itself. It is the last folly to bother about the world. One should be in love, and be happy, and –'

FRIEDA: You go too fast! Slow down!

LAWRENCE: Sorry.

Beat. She writes furiously.

FRIEDA: 'One should be in love –'?

LAWRENCE: ' – and be happy – no more. Except – except if there are *friends* to help the happiness on, so much the better. Let us be happy together.'

Beat.

FRIEDA: Go on.

He steps forward and a compelling, almost evangelical certainty enters his voice.

LAWRENCE: 'This is a most beautiful place. A tiny granite village nestling under high, shaggy moor-hills, and a big sweep of lovely sea beyond. It is five miles from St.Ives and seven miles from Penzance. It is all gorse now, flickering with flower –'

FRIEDA: Yes, I like that.

LAWRENCE: ' – and then it will be heather, and then hundreds of foxgloves. It is the best place I have been in, I think.'

FRIEDA: Good.

As he continues, the larger cottage next door becomes slowly visible, and the small 'tower'room beneath the crenellated roof. KATHERINE enters the room, dressed for travelling, carrying a small suitcase.

LAWRENCE: 'I call it already Katherine's house. Katherine's Tower. It is very old, native to the earth, like rock, yet dry and all in the light of the hills and the sea. It is only twelve strides from our house to yours,we can talk from the windows. And besides us, only the gorse, and the fields, and the lambs skipping and hopping like anything, and the seagulls fighting with the ravens, and sometimes a fox, and a ship on the sea.'

FRIEDA: Now say how cheap it is.

LAWRENCE: 'You must come, and we will live here a long time, very cheaply.'

FRIEDA: And again repeat how cheap.

LAWRENCE: 'For we must live somewhere, and it is so free and beautiful, and it will cost so very little.'

FRIEDA: Good.

LAWRENCE: 'And don't talk any more of treacheries and so on. Henceforward, let us take each other on trust. We count you as our only two tried friends, our real and permanent blood-kin. I know – I *know* we shall be happy this summer.'

Lights fade on FRIEDA and LAWRENCE. KATHERINE takes off her hat. There is a nail in the wall. She hangs it on the nail.

Scene ends.

SCENE TWO

KATHERINE is in the Tower room as before, looking out of the window. LAWRENCE enters quietly. He observes her for a moment.

LAWRENCE: Well, Mansfield. Will it do?

She spins around.

KATHERINE: Lorenzo…what a darling you are.

LAWRENCE: Thought this was the room for you.

KATHERINE: It's perfect – perfect.

LAWRENCE: And I know downstairs still needs a bit of work, but now Jack's here –

KATHERINE: Jack Murry?

LAWRENCE: Now now, Mansfield.

KATHERINE: Have you ever seen him wield a hammer?

LAWRENCE: You're a wicked woman.

KATHERINE: Really, dear, you'll wonder how you ever coped without him. What about the neighbours?

LAWRENCE: Them next door?

KATHERINE: That's right.

LAWRENCE: Well, what about them?

KATHERINE: Are they trouble?

LAWRENCE: Absolutely. He's a filthy pacifist and she's a filthy Hun.

KATHERINE: I'd heard he was a filthy *novelist.*

LAWRENCE: He's that as well.

KATHERINE: By all accounts his last book was obscene.

LAWRENCE: 'Spiritually and morally reprehensible', they say.

KATHERINE: Sounds like essential reading on the Cornish coast.

LAWRENCE: And 'windy, tedious, boring and nauseating' to boot.

KATHERINE: Oh no, Lorenzo, who said that?

LAWRENCE: Robert Lynd, *Daily News.* Page 5, paragraph 4. *The Rainbow* – first review. Peculiarly hard to forget.

KATHERINE: Robert Lynd – the man's an idiot. He's no idea.

LAWRENCE: At any rate, we're here now. I don't seem to mind so much, here.

KATHERINE: And the wisdom of Robert Lynd is soaking up cheap vinegar in pie-and-eel shops nationwide.

LAWRENCE: Queer thing is, I really don't much mind. One looks at this landscape – the crags, the rocks, the great primeval cliffs and the lovely sweep of the sea – and the things that break one's heart in London don't seem to matter at all. London vanishes in a puff of smoke – Bohemia and Bloomsbury are extinct. Nothing matters but this, and the grass, and the animals roaming about.

KATHERINE: It was the same in Bandol, too. Even the war felt remote.

LAWRENCE: Even in France?

KATHERINE: The day they attacked Verdun, I finished my new story. Jack went to the village and bought a bottle of Maderia to celebrate –

LAWRENCE: Madeira!

KATHERINE: …was all he could find. We drank the lot and sang through the entire score of *Hello Ragtime* very loudly on the terrace. The next morning the front page of the newspaper was like an accusation – how could we be so carefree? But we were.

LAWRENCE: You were happy. Why in God's name shouldn't you be?

JACK: (*Off.*) Tig! Where are you, Tig!

KATHERINE: (*Calling.*) In my Tower, darling! (*To LAWRENCE.*) Well, indeed. And yet one feels one shouldn't.

LAWRENCE: That's the hypocrisy of this blasted war. We didn't wage it, we're not behind it, and yet we're expected to pack up our troubles, our joys and, most importantly, our *principles*, and sacrific ourselves wholeheartedly to this idiot government and its –

JACK enters with a knock.

JACK: Frieda says, and I quote: you've to 'stop banging on at Katherine about the war, Lloyd George and the idiot government and come at once downstairs to where the chicken you've half-cooked is sitting blackening in the range.' We were next door hunting for the gramophone.

LAWRENCE: Was that word-for-word?

JACK: (*With a little bow.*) But of course.

LAWRENCE: Of course. Brain like the bloody Bodleian.

JACK: (*Looking round.*) I say, look at this.

KATHERINE: Isn't it splendid?

JACK: Well you've done it now, old chap. You've spoilt her for life. I'll never persuade her to live in a bug infested Chelsea fleapit again.

LAWRENCE: Christ, I'd forgotten, that place of yours –

KATHERINE: Don't, please, don't!

JACK: The rooms weren't bad, though.

KATHERINE: If you're partial to huge black cockroaches.

LAWRENCE: When we got back from Lerici and found you two poor buggers there –

KATHERINE: I can smell kerosene and sulphur at the thought of it.

JACK: It worked though, didn't it, that frightful sulphur?

KATHERINE: I'll say so. Cockroach corpses strewn across the floor…

LAWRENCE: Mansfield, my lass, you'll never live like that again. We'll make sure of it, won't we, Jack?

KATHERINE: Oh, promise me we won't, however poor and desperate we get.

LAWRENCE: Not here we won't. Everything's so cheap and fresh and good. The vegetables I planted when we first arrived are coming through already and it's only April. We live on good farm bread, eggs, butter, honey, the odd chicken if we can get it. We've never got by so well on so little. And sometimes –

JACK: Look, speaking of chickens –

KATHERINE: Are you going to tell a joke, my love?

JACK: It's only Frieda was quite serious –

LAWRENCE laughs and ruffles his hair affectionately.

LAWRENCE: He thinks the fearful Hun might shoot the messenger. Come on, then, come downstairs with me. There's a fire. I'll fetch some tea – or wine.

LAWRENCE goes downstairs and exits into the kitchen.

JACK: Feeling better, Tig?

KATHERINE: Poor boy, was I a devil of a travelling companion?

JACK: Well, it was a devil of a journey.

KATHERINE: Oh… *God*!

JACK: What?

KATHERINE: Why can't you just say: 'yes, you were Satan incarnate'. We both know it's true. I was absolutely vile and hateful to you from the minute that we left the villa. Why don't you say it?

JACK: I can't see why it matters now. We're here.

KATHERINE: Because – because then everything gets put away – shut away – as though it didn't happen –

Enter LAWRENCE downstairs with a bottle of wine.

LAWRENCE: (*Calling.*) Come on, you two! It's warmer down here.

JACK: (*Calling.*) On our way!

KATHERINE: (*Suddenly, to JACK.*) I'm sorry, darling.

JACK: That's all right. You're tired, that's all.

KATHERINE: Odd thing is, I'm not. I know I ought to be.

JACK: (*Yawning, laughing.*) Well, I am.

KATHERINE: My love. You're never more exactly like a boy than when you yawn. When you screw up your eyes like that I can see you at four – five – six – oh, don't grow up too quickly.

JACK: Never.

KATHERINE: Promise?

LAWRENCE: (*Off.*) Murrys! Get yourselves down here! On the double!

JACK: Race you.

Pushing past each other, laughing, they go downstairs. LAWRENCE is pouring out glasses of wine.

LAWRENCE: I suppose I should mention we're under surveillance.

JACK: Are we?

KATHERINE: How thrilling!

LAWRENCE: Yes, the local bobby pops in regularly for a 'chat'.

JACK: What does he want to chat about?

LAWRENCE: Oh, the unseasonable weather, the foxes on the moors. What in hell we think we're doing here.

KATHERINE: No – surely not?

LAWRENCE: He doesn't say as much. And he's a decent fellow really. He's been rejected twice for military service – got astigmatism. So he's stuck as a policeman in Zennor with nowt to police.

KATHERINE: So he's policing you.

LAWRENCE: There has been – some suspicion. Couple of cargo ships went down last month between Land's End and here. There's talk of German U-boats. Sometimes the cliffs are crawling with coast-watchers like lice.

KATHERINE: Fearfully hard on Frieda, all this anti-German feeling.

LAWRENCE: Well, I tell her to pretends to be Swiss, but she will keep talking about bratwurst and knackwurst and

23

weisswurst. If she weren't so interested in sausage meat we might be less conspicuous.

JACK: So what does he say, this policeman?

LAWRENCE: (*Bad Cornish accent.*) 'Excuse me, sir. I've just a few enquiries to make.'

KATHERINE: Is he a Welshman?

LAWRENCE: Watch it, Mansfield.

JACK: What does he enquire?

LAWRENCE: Oh, we've quite a routine going, he and I. He asks to see my papers, and I show him them. He wonders if my parents were both born in England, and I reassure him that they were. He asks if I've been called up yet to Bodmin and I tell him, yes, I had a medical last month – a bloody hellish one at that –

JACK: (*Anxiously.*) Really? Was it?

LAWRENCE: I'm telling you, Murry. Steer clear as long as you can.

JACK: What did they do to you?

LAWRENCE: Stripped me naked, humiliated me almost to death, kept me overnight in a vile barracks like a prison camp, and then sent me packing, with a big red R for Rejected.

JACK: Horrible.

LAWRENCE: Of course, one wants to say, you can't *reject* me from a club I never asked to join, but it's not worth it. I was just glad to be a free man in the fresh air.

KATHERINE: Well, Jack'll be all right, he's got a doctor's note. He's officially excused from all rough games including hockey and trench-warfare.

LAWRENCE: Glad to hear it. Weak chest?

JACK: Query TB.

LAWRENCE: Really!

JACK: I'm fine, of course, only I had that bout of pleurisy last autumn and the quack in London thought I was 'susceptible'.

LAWRENCE: Well, jolly good. They don't want you at the Front.

KATHERINE: Not unless they're awfully keen for Germany to win.

LAWRENCE: Sometimes I think *I'm* awfully keen for Germany to win –

KATHERINE: Lorenzo, shush!

LAWRENCE: It's true!

Laughter. FRIEDA enters, carrying a small portable gramophone.

FRIEDA: What is he saying now? Has he been telling tales about me? I don't care! I could hear you laughing through the walls. How wonderful, I thought, we don't need music now. We are the music!

She puts the gramophone down and embraces KATHERINE. She peers over her shoulder into the kitchen.

Is the meat done yet? How good it smells!

LAWRENCE: It's not quite done.

JACK: I hope you haven't spent a fortune on us, you two.

LAWRENCE: Well, from now on we can live on cigarettes and turnip-ends if you like but tonight we've to eat and be merry. It's a celebration.

FRIEDA: Besides which, Jack, they gave to us a chicken from the farm.

LAWRENCE: So they did. The Hockings at Lower Tregerthen, the farmstead down the lane. They're generous folk.

FRIEDA: You worked for it!

LAWRENCE: Not *work*. Sometimes I teach a bit of French to William Henry Hocking and his younger brother. Now *he's* an interesting fellow, William; you'll meet him. Very Cornish and a farmer to the core, but brooding, with a curious mind.

KATHERINE: And do they always pay in poultry?

LAWRENCE: Not just poultry: eggs, butter, milk! Country life, you see, Mansfield. You'd not get that in Russell Square.

JACK: Too many poets –

KATHERINE: And not enough hens.

JACK: Sounds like a proverb.

KATHERINE: Too many poets spoil the –

FRIEDA: This hen *will* be spoiled if you don't see to her, Lorenzo.

LAWRENCE: Yes, all right.

JACK: Can't we give you a hand, Lorenzo?

LAWRENCE: Come and watch the potatoes if you like. They should be nearly done.

FRIEDA: Jack, darling, you are honoured! He never lets anyone help.

LAWRENCE: Don't catch you complaining much, my lady.

JACK stands. LAWRENCE thwacks him across the back of the legs with a tea-towel.

JACK: Ouch, you bastard!

FRIEDA: Lorenzo!

LAWRENCE: Sign of affection, isn't it, Murry?

JACK: (*Snatching the tea-towel.*) Utter devotion, Lorenzo.

They chase each other outside, thwacking wildly at each other. The women look at each other, amused. During the following, they set the table.

FRIEDA: Sometimes I wonder why I mourn my children when I have this giant baby for a husband.

KATHERINE: How *are* the children? Do you hear from them?

FRIEDA: I had some photographs from Ernest's sister. No letter, but at least the photographs. It's good of her. She is a bitch, but still it's good of her.

KATHERINE: Might I see them, the pictures?

FRIEDA: Katherine, how kind you are, you always take such interest. I will never forget how you went that day to the school for me.

KATHERINE: Gosh, that was nothing. I was glad to speak to them; I only wished I could do more. It seems absurd that Ernest can keep them from you. It's 1916, for heaven's sake. You're not Anna Karenina.

FRIEDA: But even now, if Ernest changed his mind –

KATHERINE: Do you think he might?

FRIEDA: Well, it would be no use. Lorenzo doesn't want them.

KATHERINE: But surely he –

A burst of laughter from outside. FRIEDA glances at the door.

FRIEDA: But what of you, Katinka? What gossip do you have to tell me?

KATHERINE: Not a great deal, really. George Bowden still refuses to divorce me.

FRIEDA: Does he?

KATHERINE: It's awfully frustrating. I know I treated him shamefully –

FRIEDA: Of course you did! To marry him and leave him in one afternoon!

KATHERINE: But it was almost ten years ago, Frieda! He's scarcely set eyes on me since, and he knows I live with Jack – that to all intents and purposes I'm Jack's wife. So why in the world does he want to stay married to me? He doesn't even know me.

FRIEDA: Perhaps he likes to be the husband of a famous writer.

KATHERINE: I'm hardly *that*. But in the meantime, Jack and I can't marry. And the time goes by –

FRIEDA: Yes, you must, you must have children while you can.

KATHERINE: But Frieda, tell me more about *yours* –

The men are heard returning, laughing. FRIEDA holds up her hand.

FRIEDA: Sh-sh. We'll talk of it later. He hates me to talk of it.

KATHERINE frowns. FRIEDA puts a record on the gramophone.

We'll listen only to happy music tonight. We shan't have any melancholy, not tonight when we're so glad. There – that's nice. (*She sings along, guessing at the words.*) I love 'I Love A Piano'…

Music plays. JACK and LAWRENCE reappear, somewhat battered.

KATHERINE: Were you wounded, sweetheart? Will you live?

JACK: I've got a fearful stitch.

FRIEDA: Come, come, Jack, sit and rest. (*To LAWRENCE.*) What's wrong with you?

LAWRENCE: (*Wincing.*) Bashed my knee on the gate.

FRIEDA: Good, it serves you right. I don't think dancing on the grass with dishcloths will make good our reputation in the village.

LAWRENCE: Why, since when did spies dance about with dishcloths?

KATHERINE: But surely they don't really think you're spies.

LAWRENCE: Why not? Folk are forever thinking I'm a spy.

FRIEDA: It's true. When we went first to Germany together I took him to a little park in Metz –

LAWRENCE: That's right –

FRIEDA: And we were lying in the grass and all at once there comes a soldier –

LAWRENCE: And announces he's been listening to our conversation and deduced that I'm a spy.

JACK: What had you been talking about?

LAWRENCE: Sweet bloody nothings, what'd you think!

FRIEDA: I don't remember that we *talked* at all.

LAWRENCE: We were hardly exchanging state secrets, at any rate. And there's this soldier desperate to arrest me and inform her father, who already wants me clapped in irons –

KATHERINE: And did he?

FRIEDA: No, I cried and cried until he let us go.

LAWRENCE: P'raps I *ought* to be a spy. I might be more successful at it.

FRIEDA: But here, of course, it is me who they suspect. I am the Hunwife. A pariah, I am.

LAWRENCE: She's exaggerating.

FRIEDA: No I don't! Yesterday I was in Zennor and I saw the children coming from the church after the Easter sermon. And a little boy was on his own just waiting by the gate. And he begins to tell me all about the Easter story and then suddenly from nowhere – snap! The mother snatches him away as if he has been talking with a tramp.

KATHERINE: Frieda, how hateful.

LAWRENCE: What were you dressed in?

FRIEDA: Nothing! My brown skirt!

LAWRENCE: Only she's provoked the wrath of the clergy by wearing red stockings. Apparently her legs have been the subject of several sermons.

JACK: You're not serious.

FRIEDA: But absolutely true.

KATHERINE: For wearing them to church?

FRIEDA: No, not even to church, just in the streets.

JACK: But this is priceless.

LAWRENCE: Yes, one has to laugh –

FRIEDA: *He* laughs, but then he makes it worse by sitting in the Tinner's Arms and bellowing about the war –

LAWRENCE: Oh, here we go…

FRIEDA: And they don't like it! Well, they *don't*, Lorenzo. Their sons, their brothers are off fighting and they come in only for a quiet drink and have to listen to him preaching on and on – 'this war, it is a blasphemy against life itself –'

LAWRENCE: All right, all right.

FRIEDA: 'A blasphemy that we are all commiting every day!' No wonder they don't like us.

LAWRENCE: There are plenty of decent folk who *do* like us. The Hockings, and the Berrymans and plenty more.

FRIEDA: Anyway, besides, *you* are here now. We won't care a pin for them now we have you.

LAWRENCE: And speaking of which, we ought to have a toast. Where's the bottle? Let's have a toast.

He fills their glasses.

To Rananim.

FRIEDA: Oh, not your Rananim again.

LAWRENCE: Yes, Rananim, the magic island of my dreams, to which the four of us are forever sailing in my mind. I have only to close my eyes and I can see our schooner ploughing through the waves, dodging U-boats with the cunning of a shark and –

KATHERINE / JACK: – sharks with the cunning of a U-boat…

They look at each other and laugh.

LAWRENCE: That's it! Murry, you're manning the rigging. Mansfield, you're up in the crow's nest.

FRIEDA: What about me? Where am I?

LAWRENCE: In the hold, bound and gagged –

FRIEDA: I'm not!

LAWRENCE: Up on deck in the moonlight with me.

JACK: All right for some!

KATHERINE: Would *you* like to be in the moonlight with Lorenzo, pet?

JACK: I'd sooner that than manning any rigging.

FRIEDA: Lorenzo, cannot *you* man the rigging? Jack would be much nicer in the moonlight than you.

LAWRENCE: I've no doubt he would.

KATHERINE: Yes, Jack *is* rather nice in the moonlight, only he's fearfully scared of night-creatures. He'd be squealing and hopping about like anything –

JACK: Tig, that's slander –

LAWRENCE: What sort of creatures?

KATHERINE: Bats and things.

JACK: What rot!

KATHERINE: You know you are.

FRIEDA: (*To JACK.*) I don't mind, I will protect you from the bats.

LAWRENCE: That's settled then. Frieda can fend off Murry's bats, whilst Mansfield and I do the legwork. We're off, my hearties. Here's to Rananim!

ALL: To Rananim!

LAWRENCE: Wherever it may turn out to be – Mexico, perhaps, or Florida – one day I know we'll get there.

They drink.

So. Secondly, and more sensibly –

KATHERINE: Oh no, don't be more sensible!

LAWRENCE: To Jack's Dostoevsky book and Katherine's story.

FRIEDA: Jack's book and Katherine's story! Can we read them?

KATHERINE: Read his, it's tremendously good.

FRIEDA: How clever you both are!

JACK: Well, let's not speak too soon…

KATHERINE: Why? It's brilliant and you know it. It's the best thing he's done.

LAWRENCE: And yours?

KATHERINE: Mine isn't ready yet. It's just a sort of prelude.

FRIEDA: To what?

KATHERINE smiles and shakes her head.

LAWRENCE: A novel?

JACK: It ought to be a novel. It's absolutely first-chop –

KATHERINE: (*Waving it away.*) Oh, aren't we all just too too talented!

FRIEDA: And your new book, Lorenzo.

LAWRENCE: Eh?

JACK: Lorenzo! Have you started a new one?

FRIEDA: Yes, his sequel for *The Rainbow.*

LAWRENCE: I've not started anything yet.

FRIEDA: Oh, but he will, any day. He has all the thoughts, the ideas –

LAWRENCE: I haven't –

FRIEDA: But me, I am not gifted like the rest of you. It may be you'll have to throw me overboard…or eat me.

33

KATHERINE: That's not true. Beatrice showed me the jacket you made for her baby and I've never seen anything so delicate and lovely in my life. I said to Jack at once – didn't I, Jag – that when the stork finally condescends to hover, our hordes of offspring are to be entirely kitted out by you.

JACK: Frieda, you're commissioned. Hordes of romper-suits.

FRIEDA: You are very kind, but I don't mind. My role is different.

LAWRENCE: She's my muse.

FRIEDA: My 'role' is in the hay.

LAWRENCE: Yes, all right, all right.

FRIEDA: (*Delighted with her joke.*) My roll is in the hay!

LAWRENCE: There's one more thing I want to say –

FRIEDA: Go on, finish your speech, and let us eat.

JACK: Speech, speech!

LAWRENCE: It's not a bloody speech. I only want to say –

KATHERINE: (*To JACK.*) I'm not going to vote for him, are you?

LAWRENCE: All right, pipe down in the peanut gallery.

KATHERINE: My money's on Lloyd George.

LAWRENCE: All right, all right!

Laughter, then they settle and become attentive.

Mansfield, Murry. I want to thank you. For trusting us. For coming. You're the only friends left for us now. And we'll stand by you as long as we live.

Beat.

Remember the day it all began, and we stood up on Parliament Hill in the sun? It didn't seem possible, did it, then – in the sun, with the dogs and the children running about. It'll be two years in August. Nothing but destruction. So much lost and nothing gained. And of course, your brother, Katherine.

FRIEDA: A tragedy, it was. A lovely handsome boy. We thought of you.

KATHERINE: Thank you.

Beat.

LAWRENCE: But imagine. What a wonder it would be, if at this black, this terrifying point in history – in spite of the despicable mob mentality that spews up from the gutters and threatens the very heart of England more than Germany ever would or could – in spite of the grotesque incompetence of our government and –

FRIEDA: And this he says is not a speech?

LAWRENCE: – in spite of the foul mendacity of the press – in spite of the inexorable forward-march of the great death-spitting machine of war –

FRIEDA: This is what he does! This is exactly –

LAWRENCE: – in spite of all of that, if we four could come together to make something good and positive and true. In this rugged little corner of our country, this wild, beautiful, unsullied place, if we could make a true *community*, of real friends who love each other. To live a free and simple life, and work, and farm the land, and write, and talk, and love each other – and no more. It is, I believe, the only way – the only way to rise up like the phoenix from the ashes of what England has become.

FRIEDA: The phoenix, always he brings in his blessed phoenix. If it isn't Rananim, it is the phoenix.

35

LAWRENCE: It's my totem. When the phoenix is hurt, he gives birth to himself again from the wound. He doesn't die of it, he doesn't let it kill him, but *from the pain* he recreates himself, renewed and healed.

KATHERINE: I like that. Renewal – at whatever cost. I'll drink to that.

LAWRENCE: (*Raising his glass.*) Renewal!

ALL: To renewal!

They drink.

FRIEDA: Here's to *us.*

ALL: To us!

They drink.

JACK: To friendship!

LAWRENCE: Yes!

ALL: To friendship!

They drink.

KATHERINE: (*Softly.*) 'Now I will believe that there are unicorns, that in Arabia there is one tree, the phoenix' throne; one phoenix, at this hour reigning there.'

FRIEDA: We need more music. And the food, Lorenzo.

She goes to the gramophone and changes the record.

LAWRENCE: That's marvellous – is it *Othello*?

JACK: *The Tempest.* Act Three, Scene Three.

LAWRENCE: Say it again, will you, Mansfield?

KATHERINE: 'Now I will believe that there are unicorns, that in Arabia there is one tree, the phoenix' throne, one phoenix, at this hour reigning there.'

LAWRENCE: Marvellous! 'Now I will believe –' Just say it one more time –

FRIEDA: Lorenzo, that godforsaken chicken will be rising like your phoenix from its ashes if you do not go and –

LAWRENCE: Hold on! Listen!

FRIEDA: What? What is it?

LAWRENCE: Sshh! The recording – listen!

Everyone listens.

FRIEDA: What is it?

LAWRENCE: You put it on!

FRIEDA: I put the first I found –

LAWRENCE: It's Rananim – that song Koteliansky sings – with 'Rananim' in it – that's where I got the word from – it's that Hebrew song he sings! Remember, Jack? Kot sang it to us on his birthday when we walked back from the Café Royal – turn it louder!

FRIEDA turns it up.

KATHERINE: It *is* beautiful...

FRIEDA: I like Billy Murray, don't you? Do you know *I Love A Piano*?

JACK: I remember. 'Rejoice', it means, Kot said. Or 'celebrate' –

LAWRENCE: Yes! It's a sign! A blessing! It's deliciously symbolic –

FRIEDA: Never mind symbolic, we are *hungry*! We can't live on signs and blessings!

LAWRENCE: Good God, woman, do you think of nothing but your stomach?

FRIEDA: It is nearly midnight! They've been travelling all day!

LAWRENCE: Well, can't *you* get up from your massive –

FRIEDA: (*Rising.*) Do you really want me to?

LAWRENCE: No, no! Sit down! I'll do it!

He goes quickly into the kitchen.

FRIEDA: See, he is just like a child that has to be manipulated. Sit, sit anywhere. Here, Jack, sit by me. How handsome he is, Katherine, how really very fine! But you were always handsome, Jack, only when we met you, you were such a boy!

JACK: D'you know, it only seems five minutes since the four of us were sitting on that bus in Soho –

He breaks off as LAWRENCE enters with a roasted chicken on a plate. It is totally blackened. They all stare at it.

Beat.

KATHERINE starts to laugh. After a moment, they all join in.

Scene ends.

SCENE THREE

Tower Cottage. LAWRENCE and JACK are laying linoleum on the floor.

LAWRENCE: See, Jack, you're full of promise, almost more than any man I know, but not a seed of it has flowered in you and won't until you realise that your craving for the personal'll get you nowhere. Making choices out of the desire for love and reassurance will only make you impotent in the face of the world.

JACK: But surely, Lorenzo, if one *feels* love –

LAWRENCE: (*Holding out his hand.*) Hammer. Oh, yes, *feel* it, by all means. Seek intimacy with Katherine if you want to –

JACK: Why, of course –

LAWRENCE: – but in your friendships with men – with me, for instance – there ought to be a greater goal; a separate and impersonal intention. Our bond must necessarily be active, channelled into purpose – not just keeping company for want of sentimental validation. It isn't worth a bean unless its purpose-driven, towards a cause that matters. Do you see that?

JACK: Yes –

LAWRENCE: And don't say yes to me because you want to please me, or to reassure yourself of my love for you. You know that I love you, so for Christ's sake don't ask for proof like a woman does.

JACK: No, I didn't mean to –

LAWRENCE: Say yes because you believe in me, because you want to work with me towards something impersonal and important, something greater than the sum of our parts. Say yes because you commit to being my disciple – because you're with me for the Revolution – because if I carve out the way, you'll be prepared to build the temple. Want some beer?

JACK: (*Weakly.*) Why not?

LAWRENCE goes into the kitchen. He returns with two bottles of beer.

LAWRENCE: At this rate we'll be finished by tonight. And then tomorrow we can do the cliff walk to St Ives. It might even be warm enough to bathe. (*Raising his bottle; a now-familiar toast.*) To us; to Rananim!

JACK: To Rananim!

They clink their bottles.

LAWRENCE: Did you know that the Italians take it terribly to heart if you don't look 'em in the eye when you drink a toast? They say it's bad luck not to.

JACK: Why?

LAWRENCE: I don't know – no more do they, I expect. But we don't want bad luck, do we. Come on – look at me. To Rananim!

JACK: To Rananim!

Looking at each other, they clink bottles.

Now don't break contact. It's quite a thing to meet another fellow's gaze full-on. There's something terrible and strangely wonderful about it. We hardly ever do it, we're afraid of it. The Cornishmen are worse, just look at William Henry. Those bright black eyes that flicker at you like an animal's, and then he looks away. No – don't break contact. Why is it, d'you suppose, Jack? What are we afraid of?

JACK: It's our English awkwardness, our born-and-bred self-consciousness. There's no escape from it.

LAWRENCE: Why isn't there? Why can't we just be free and unselfconscious like the Latins are? Keep contact! What poison in our blood makes us this way?

JACK: All I know is that I've been utterly, wretchedly self-conscious since the moment I was conscious at all. I've never for the slightest instant been free of it, even as a little chap of four or five. I'd give anything to be. *You* seem wonderfully unselfconscious to me.

LAWRENCE: Do I, really?

JACK: God, of course you do! And – and when I'm with you, I – why, I feel freer than I've ever felt with anyone.

LAWRENCE: And I with you.

Beat. JACK laughs gently and looks away.

JACK: Sorry, Lorenzo. I'd fare very badly in Italy.

LAWRENCE pats him affectionately.

LAWRENCE: Don't worry, so did I. In Lerici I tried to pass myself off as one of them, tearing the buttons off my shirt and embracing all the shopkeepers, but in the end it was hopeless. The awful truth is that I'm English to the core. And I love England – but I wish to God I wasn't bloody English.

JACK: Do you still love it? The war hasn't spoiled it for you?

LAWRENCE: Out there, I love. Hills, grass, gorse, hedgerows, mice and birds. Just anything that isn't bloody human. Did I tell you that we see a fox from time to time? Just standing by the outhouse, looking at us, with her fine intelligent muzzle and her white throat and her brush like a flame. Such beauty. *She's* not afraid to look one in the eye. Sling us that bag of nails, will you?

JACK is lost in thought.

Jack?

JACK: Sorry –

LAWRENCE: Where'd you go?

JACK: What? When?

LAWRENCE: You were a world away.

JACK: Oh… I was thinking about Katherine.

LAWRENCE: What about her?

JACK: That she's not frightened, either. To look one in the eye.

LAWRENCE: That's right, she isn't, is she? Nor is Frieda. But then, you see, they're neither of them English.

JACK: Whereas you and I, old boy, worse luck…

He throws him the bag of nails. LAWRENCE catches it. A beat.

LAWRENCE: Why do you look so anxious when you think of Katherine? It's not that Carco business –

JACK: No. That's over.

LAWRENCE: You two seem all right.

JACK: We are. It isn't that. It's just –

LAWRENCE: Go on.

JACK: In Bandol, you see, she was writing ferociously. It simply poured from her as though she couldn't stop. And in spite of everything – her brother, and the war – she was happy. We were happy together.

LAWRENCE: Oh, God, this is my fault. I went and spoiled the idyll.

JACK: No! You know that isn't true – in any case, we had to leave. If we'd stayed a minute longer I'd have been banged up as a deserter. But somehow, she convinced herself that all her creativity was bound up with the place. Of course I said it wasn't; how could it be? Only it does seem rum that since we left –

LAWRENCE: What, she's not writing?

JACK: Says she can't.

LAWRENCE: But you've just got here! It takes time to settle somewhere new. I've hardly written anything myself, I was so ill when we arrived, and then I had that bloody palsy and I couldn't hold a pen. The odd thing is, it doesn't seem to matter, here. I work at the garden instead, or walk to the sea and watch the crabs in the rockpools.

JACK: But you write every day.

LAWRENCE: It's beginning to come.

JACK: She'll be wretched, you see, if she can't.

LAWRENCE: Well, that's her battle, and it's bloody, but you can't let it destroy you. I know what it's like and you have to resist it. You've to make yourself separate, hard and gem-like –

JACK: But I can't bear her to be unhappy. The truth is that I'm awfully dependent on her, and if I know she's miserable –

LAWRENCE: If she's miserable, man, it's *her* misery! For God's sake let her have it for herself. If you want to suffer, buy a newspaper, read about what's happening in Dublin, read about Verdun. Christ, there's plenty to be miserable about if you want to be –

JACK: I don't –

LAWRENCE: – but don't be such a fool as to infect yourself with misery in the name of love. We have to, we must learn to love without *becoming* the other person! Yes, sympathise, by all means, but don't empathise to the point of self-extinction! What's the use in that? Well, tell me, what's the use?

JACK: No, there is no use.

LAWRENCE: You're simply *both* destroyed. D'you see?

JACK: Yes. Yes, it is rather hopeless.

LAWRENCE: This is why a man must have a male companion as well as a wife. Because you and I can love each other without this infernal abnegation of the self, this fatal acquiescence of one's individual consciousness to the other person.

He lays his hand on JACK's arm and speaks with great gentleness.

Don't suffer for Katherine. She won't thank you for it. Leave her be, and she'll forget herself and start to write again. And be as happy as she was in France. You'll see.

JACK: Do you really think so?

LAWRENCE: I'm quite certain of it.

JACK: God, I must say, it's a hell of a relief to talk to you about it.

LAWRENCE: You should always tell me things. Don't hide anything, and I'll not hide anything from you. We should promise each other that, we should swear it.

JACK: Absolutely.

LAWRENCE suddenly starts up, his face alight.

LAWRENCE: I say, Jack, d'you know what we should do? We should swear a pact, a *Blutbruderschaft*, like the old German knights used to do.

JACK: What sort of pact?

LAWRENCE: You know, make a cut in their arms and mix the blood.

JACK: A cut?

LAWRENCE: And swear to be true to one another all their lives. To love one another implicitly and finally, without any possibility of going back. Shall we do it, Jack? Let's do it, shall we?

JACK: Now?

LAWRENCE: Why not? Sling me that grouting-knife.

JACK: This? It's got an awful lot of grout –

LAWRENCE: Good God, man, give it here.

He takes the knife and wipes it with his handkerchief.

That'll do. Come on. Let's swear to stand by each other – to be faithful and true – ultimately and infallibly – without any possibility of ever taking back. Roll up your sleeve.

JACK: Look, I don't know if –

LAWRENCE: It's all right, I don't mean any sort of syrupy emotionalism. Just an impersonal union that leaves one free. Here, I'll go first. You make the wound.

He rolls up his sleeve and profers the knife.

JACK: I – make the wound?

LAWRENCE: Here, in the soft part, away from the vein.

JACK: Lorenzo, I –

LAWRENCE: Come on, it's just a scratch, it isn't going to hurt.

JACK takes the knife, petrified.

Go on, man, do it! If you love me, do it.

JACK hovers.

What is it? Don't you love me?

JACK: Yes, of course I do.

LAWRENCE: Then what are you waiting for?

JACK: It's just I –

LAWRENCE: (*Snapping.*) Oh, for Christ's sake, do it or I'll bloody do it for you!

JACK does it. LAWRENCE sucks in his breath, grimacing with pain.

JACK: Are you all right? You've gone awfully pale.

LAWRENCE: Quick, hold out your arm. It's best to do it fast before the blood dries up.

JACK: Is it?

LAWRENCE: Come on, quickly.

JACK holds out his arm with great reluctance. LAWRENCE readies the blade.

All right?

JACK nods. LAWRENCE brings down the knife firmly.

JACK: *Stop!*

LAWRENCE: Jesus, what is it now?

JACK: Do you think we could –

LAWRENCE: What?

JACK: I don't know, could we wait until –

LAWRENCE: *What?*

JACK: Could we wait until I understand the whole thing better?

Beat. With an effort, LAWRENCE swallows his disappointment.

LAWRENCE: Of course. Let me know when you're ready.

He binds his own arm with the handkerchief. JACK gives him an apologetic smile.

Scene ends.

SCENE FOUR

Outside the cottages. Early evening. Weak sunshine. FRIEDA is washing clothes with tremendous zest, plunging them into a bowl of soapy water and wringing them out powerfully, drops of water flying into the air. KATHERINE hangs them on the line.

FRIEDA: Katerina, you have purposely bewitched me! What do you do to me, to make me tell you all these things? And then *you*, you will not tell me anything at all!

Beat.

Well, all right, he was my cousin, and his name was Curt von Richthofen. He was a cadet at the Metz Officers school, and on Sundays he would come to us for tea. I used to stare at him across the table. He was so handsome! Tall and fair, with beautiful gleaming teeth.

KATHERINE: So what happened?

FRIEDA: Well, finally one day I took him by the hand and led him in the garden, and I pulled him down among my father's hyacinths.

KATHERINE: How old were you?

FRIEDA: Fifteen, and he was twenty-one.

KATHERINE: How marvellous!

FRIEDA: But he of course was hopelessly naïve. I had to teach him everything. 'I don't know how I am supposed to have all these tactics under my belt,' he would say, and I would say, 'darling, when I undo your belt it's not *tactics* I am looking for.'

KATHERINE: Poor Curt. You must have frightened him to death.

FRIEDA: I did! I did! So all summer we rolled in the hyacinths and fed each other big wild strawberries. Then in August, just after my birthday, he was posted to Hamburg. He gave to me a box of macaroons, each wrapped in silver tissue, and I put them underneath my bed so that my sisters wouldn't know. Then in the morning, I could not get up. I lay there in the soulsick anguish of the first love. I reached under the bed for one macaroon only, to console me, and Katherine –

KATHERINE: You ate them all.

FRIEDA: How did you guess?

KATHERINE: How many?

FRIEDA: Thirty, forty, I don't know. A pile of silver tissues.

KATHERINE: Never mind soulsick, you must have been violently ill.

FRIEDA: Of course I was. And ever since, if I am sad – I eat. If I am happy, I eat also. So I never will have your exquisite little figure, and I always will hate myself in a bathing suit, and it is all the fault of Curt von Richthofen.

KATHERINE: And did you ever see those gleaming teeth again?

FRIEDA: Never, no. Nor thought of them again until today.

KATHERINE: I'll bet he thinks of you.

FRIEDA: I bet he doesn't!

KATHERINE: Oh, he'll be married to some Gretchen or some Gudrun and believe he's splendidly content but I'll bet you anything whenever he smells hyacinths, or Gretchen serves up big wild strawberries…

FRIEDA: (*Laughs.*) But this is life, is it not, Katerina? Food and sex, sex and food. Appetite and hunger, desire and satisfaction. One forgets for a while, and then the body it reminds us – it wants things. It must be fed. This is how we know we are alive. Don't you agree?

KATHERINE: Yes, I suppose.

FRIEDA: And *now,* Miss I-Suppose…

KATHERINE: Are there more pegs?

FRIEDA: Oh, never mind your pegs! I cannot wait another minute!

KATHERINE: What?

FRIEDA: Katherine, come! You must admit, I have been very patient, have I not? And now it is your turn to talk.

KATHERINE: (*Slowly.*) Oh.

FRIEDA: Because of course Jack came to us in such a state last year. But he would not say much. Only that you were unhappy and you'd gone away to Dijon. And he mentioned someone – a man. Come, Katinka, you surely know *I* will not disapprove!

Beat. KATHERINE sighs.

KATHERINE: His name is Francis Carco. He's a writer. It was Jack who introduced us, they're old friends. We met up with him once in Paris and I liked him tremendously, but that was all. Then, last year, he began to write to me, these terribly exciting letters, and –

She breaks off momentarily.

What one has to understand is that Jack and I have a most amazing love. An absolutely pure and lovely love. And every time I think it's all coming to a frightful end, it somehow seems to reinvent itself again. And each time it astonishes me. The strength of my feeling for him.

Beat.

Of course one always wishes certain things were different, but –

FRIEDA: What things?

KATHERINE: Well, surely there are things about Lorenzo that –

FRIEDA: Yes, yes, but Jack's so lovely, such a gentleman –

KATHERINE: Oh, he's adorable, he's charming, who couldn't love Jack? Apart from all the people who can't stand him – but one can't please everybody, can one? Jack's trouble is, he tries to.

Beat.

I wish he were stronger, more carefree, *spendthrift* of himself. A man of action. What we used to call a Pa-Man, back home. The sort of man whose arms you could fly into and be quite sure that he'd make everything all right. But he's isn't. He's Jack.

FRIEDA: And Mr Francis Carco, was he a Pa-Man?

KATHERINE: (*Laughs.*) Not in the least, as it turned out. He was like a pretty girl who thought it was all a great adventure, sneaking me into the war-zone and squirrelling me away in his rooms.

FRIEDA: It was in the war-zone!

KATHERINE: Our Mr Carco's a little corporal.

FRIEDA: But how did you get past the military?

KATHERINE: An elaborate fib; an invalid aunt. Awfully handy, invalid aunts. One ought to collect them. Somehow an invalid *uncle* doesn't quite cut the mustard.

FRIEDA: And you call me brave for kissing in the hyacinths!

KATHERINE: Well, it'll make a story.

FRIEDA: But that's all – a story?

KATHERINE: (*Smiles.*) That's 'all'.

FRIEDA: And no regrets?

KATHERINE: If Jack was hurt, I'm sorry. But he knew what I was doing and not once did he try to stop me. He just stood and watched me pack, for all the world as though my mythical aunt were waiting at the station. He never said, why are you doing this? Or afterwards, asked me anything at all.

FRIEDA: He never asked what happened?

KATHERINE: Frieda, I could come to breakfast in full Maori war-dress, waving a spear and uttering fearful battle-cries, and Jack would glance up from his *Times* and tell me that we're short on damson jam.

FRIEDA: So what *did* happen?

They share a smile, a laugh.

Well, and?

KATHERINE: And, although this may seem inconceivable to you, it wasn't the important part of the adventure. It wasn't passionate or even very memorable, just natural and rather sweet. Not a huge event.

FRIEDA: Not 'huge', then?

KATHERINE: (*Pained.*) Frieda...

FRIEDA: Remember I know all about you! I know that you are not so prim!

KATHERINE: (*Glancing around.*) Sshh.

FRIEDA: How silly, that you must be always so afraid! I cannot understand why you and Jack don't just talk openly about each other's pasts as we do. Lorenzo said from the beginning that we must be open and naked before one another like Adam and Eve in the Garden of Eden.

KATHERINE: Why? Look what happened to *them*.

FRIEDA: Oh, Katherine!

KATHERINE: Besides, Jack doesn't want to know.

FRIEDA: But now you're happy, you and he?

Beat.

KATHERINE: When I heard the news about my brother, I thought – well, bang goes happiness. I'll never be happy again. But then, in Bandol, we were blissful. Nothing mattered more than where Jack had left his glasses or should we walk down to the harbour for tea or stay and cook sardines and read Keats to each other in bed.

FRIEDA: Please say that's not all you did to each other in bed.

KATHERINE: *Frieda.*

FRIEDA: Good! I am happy to know it! Lorenzo and I, however bad things get –

KATHERINE: Look, they're coming.

FRIEDA: We even did it in a tree one afternoon.

JACK: (*Off.*) Ahoy there!

FRIEDA: It was awkward, with the branches, but so fun!

JACK enters, wet-haired, with a rolled-up towel

JACK: Hey, I've finally found something I can beat Lorenzo at!

KATHERINE: Don't tell us, darling. Hide and Seek?

JACK: The man may be a poet and a prophet and the only true, original voice of his generation – he may be able to cook like Mrs Beeton and paint like Paul Gauguin and make vegetable gardens spring from the parched earth but he simply – cannot – *swim.*

LAWRENCE appears, wet-haired and breathless.

FRIEDA: Yes, it's true. He cannot swim. He splutters like a pig in the water.

LAWRENCE: But hark, what honeyed tones are these? 'He splutters like a pig in the water,' quoth the sacred priestess of the Rhine. Come here, thou luscious Hunwife –

FRIEDA: (*Shrieks.*) You're wet! Get off me!

LAWRENCE: (*Pursuing her, shouting.*) Thou glorious Brunhilde! Thou great Teutonic monument!

FRIEDA: Lorenzo, shush, we are at war with Germany –

LAWRENCE: *I'm* not at war with Germany. I'm in love with Germany.

FRIEDA: You are an idiot.

LAWRENCE: Come here, Germany. Come here.

He embraces and kisses her. KATHERINE observes them.

JACK: We saw a heron, Tig.

KATHERINE: What?

JACK: We saw a heron.

LAWRENCE is whispering something to FRIEDA. She pulls away from him, laughing. He turns to the other two.

LAWRENCE: Listen, we might go in for a bit. All right? And see you later on for supper?

JACK: Yes, fine, come over when you're ready.

LAWRENCE: What've we got left? A fair old whack of cheese, potatoes. I could do my Spanish eggs if you'd like.

FRIEDA: Oh yes! How good!

JACK: Sounds splendid.

LAWRENCE pulls playfully at the washing line.

LAWRENCE: Did you know, a week or two ago the coastguards made us move this from the other side? They thought she might be signalling to the U-boats with her smalls! I told them, Frieda hasn't any *smalls*!

FRIEDA: Shut up, you idiot.

LAWRENCE: Come on, my Hapsburg queen, my Deutschland diva!

FRIEDA: Goodbye, goodbye! See you later!

They go indoors, holding hands and laughing. JACK hangs his towel on the washing-line.

JACK: He really can't swim, you know, Tig. He flails about like a great big eel and looks as if he's drowning, but he won't stop talking, even when the water goes right over his head; he just keeps on, and comes up undefeated in the middle of a sentence. Now, where the devil did I leave my –

KATHERINE hands him his glasses.

Thanks.

KATHERINE: Do you suppose he's going to do this every night?

JACK: Do what?

KATHERINE: I mean with supper. Take command of everything like that.

JACK: But that was the arrangement, wasn't it?

KATHERINE: What was? That they should occupy our kitchen every evening like a military catering corps?

JACK: No but, *their* kitchen's hardly big enough for all of us
to –

KATHERINE: All right, but can't *we* ever make the supper?
Must they always be controlling absolutely everything?

JACK: I suppose he wants to look after us, that's all. You know
how he loves to take care of everybody, make sure –

KATHERINE: But we live here now! We live here! We're not
guests.

Beat. He watches her, troubled. She sighs and pats his shoulder.

Never mind. His Spanish eggs will doubtless be delicious
and I'll have to eat my words.

JACK: Good. You're not to leave the table till you've eaten
every one.

KATHERINE: Eggs or words?

JACK: Eggs *and* words.

They smile at each other. She shivers.

Want to go in?

KATHERINE: No – don't let's go in quite yet. Just put your
arms around me for a moment.

She leans against him and he puts his arms around her.

I'll be better when I'm writing. I know I will. It's just so
easy, with Frieda, to do nothing all day but talk. We talk
and talk and the hours slip by and suddenly it's suppertime
again. And another day's wasted, gone. It's all right for her,
this way of living suits her perfectly, but I'm not Frieda,
Jag.

JACK: Of course you're not.

KATHERINE: We're really not a bit alike.

JACK: My God, you're chalk and bloody Cheddar.

Beat. They are still for a moment, watching the evening light.

KATHERINE: (*Lightly.*) Jaggle.

JACK: Mmm?

KATHERINE: Do you find Frieda attractive?

JACK: Frieda? Golly. I suppose she is – in a certain way. Like a big, bold lionness or something. Not my type, but she's good-looking. Why?

KATHERINE: She's so *healthy.* So golden and strong. Her skin – it's so creamy and dense. I can't stop staring at it. If one were to pinch her, *hard,* or bite her, I don't believe it would leave the slightest mark.

JACK: (*Playful.*) Is this what you girls think about when we leave you on your own?

KATHERINE: Her arms and her shoulders when she wrings out the washing are so powerful, like a woman in a painting, like a Michelangelo woman. Next to hers my skin looks grey and thin, as though it's withering on my bones.

JACK: What nonsense, Tig!

KATHERINE: Sometimes I think I'm drying up, day by day, like a bit of old wood.

JACK: That's perfect rot, how can you even say it? My darling mouse, you're beautiful and delicate and fine. Good God, I'd not swap one precious inch of you for a herd of great galumphing Friedas, no matter how golden they are.

KATHERINE: Do you mean that?

JACK: Do I!

KATHERINE: Look at me, Jack. Convince me.

He takes her face in her hands and looks into her eyes.

JACK: You're the only woman, Tig. The others don't exist. You're the only woman in the world.

He plants a chaste, loving kiss on her lips.

There, you darling foolish girl. Nothing to worry about, is there?

KATHERINE: (*Faintly.*) No.

JACK: Good! Come on, let's go indoors.

He helps her up. They face each other. He grins.

Race you.

Scene ends.

SCENE FIVE

The Tower Cottage. Evening. FRIEDA, LAWRENCE, JACK and KATHERINE sit around the table, on which is an upturned hat. In front of each of them is a sheet of paper.

LAWRENCE: Right, it's very simple. We played it all the time with Ottoline at Garsington last year.

He thumps the table violently.

Christ, listen to me. 'We played it all the time with Ottoline at Garsington last year.' It's sickening. I sound like bloody one of *them.*

FRIEDA: Oh, stop it!

LAWRENCE: What?

FRIEDA: Don't pretend you don't want to be one of them!

LAWRENCE: I bloody don't!

KATHERINE: Next thing you'll be taking tea with Leonard and Virginia –

JACK: And playing croquet on the lawn with Bertie Russell.

LAWRENCE: God forbid.

FRIEDA: He'd love it! Half of him wants only to be clutched to the velvet bosom of Bloomsbury but his other half must still pretend to be the coalminer's son with soot on his face and a lamp in his hand and –

KATHERINE: (*Aside, to LAWRENCE.*) A canary?

LAWRENCE: (*To KATHERINE.*) Singing in my ear...

FRIEDA: And *Lady* Ottoline Morrell likes any game where she can be Lorenzo's partner and make gu-gu eyes at him –

LAWRENCE: Well, she's not here now, so you can shut up about it.

JACK: Teach us how to play, Lorenzo.

LAWRENCE: Right. We each think up ten names and put them in the hat.

FRIEDA: But fold them, tear the paper into strips and fold them.

LAWRENCE: Obviously.

FRIEDA: No, not obviously!

JACK: Ought they to be famous people or just ones we know?

LAWRENCE: Either – both –

FRIEDA: As long as all of us know who they are. Lorenzo always puts explorers and such people that he knows I cannot guess.

LAWRENCE: Then we split up into pairs. Say you went first, Jack. You pick a name from the hat and you've a minute to

describe the person to your partner, till your partner gets
it –

FRIEDA: So you cannot say the name, but you give clues, such
as –

LAWRENCE: Am I explaining this or you?

JACK: So for example, if I picked out – 'Frieda Lawrence' –

FRIEDA: You'd say, 'Blonde woman in this room' –

LAWRENCE: Or, 'Great fat Hun', whichever you prefer.

KATHERINE: Lorenzo!

FRIEDA: I don't bother, Katherine, his insults do not interest
me.

LAWRENCE: So you get as many names as you can before the
minute's up, and then the other team have their go. We
keep going till we've emptied the hat and at the end we
count up the bits of paper.

JACK: And if there's a name we don't recognise – ?

LAWRENCE: If you can't describe the person, back in the hat
they go.

JACK: Righto.

LAWRENCE: All clear? Right. Ten names each.

*Quiet concentration as they think up names, write them and tear
up the papers.*

JACK: (*Quietly, to himself.*) Funny how names just pop into one's
head…seemingly random but…

*LAWRENCE finishes first. He scoops up his papers and puts them
in the hat.*

LAWRENCE: Come on, you lot!

He goes into the kitchen.

FRIEDA: See how competitive he is become. Even when it's just us two at chess or cribbage he is quite possessed. And if he loses – well, you do not want to see how quite insane he –

LAWRENCE returns with a bottle of wine.

LAWRENCE: Stop bloody gassing and get on with it.

KATHERINE: Done! In you go.

She tips her names into the hat.

LAWRENCE: Good lass. You and me versus Frieda and Murry?

KATHERINE: Why not.

FRIEDA: Oh, then poor Jack is stuck with me!

JACK: Poor Jack would be perfectly honoured.

LAWRENCE: If you still feel like that in half an hour, I'll eat the hat.

KATHERINE: Ah, now, talking of eating –

FRIEDA: Yes?

KATHERINE: Tomorrow night, you have to let us cook, Lorenzo. We insist. You've made more than enough delicious meals and we've just sat and lapped them up –

LAWRENCE: But it's no trouble, I enjoy it.

KATHERINE: But tomorrow, it's our turn.

LAWRENCE: Of course, if you want.

KATHERINE: Then that's settled!

LAWRENCE: Although it is Friday tomorrow.

KATHERINE: Friday?

LAWRENCE: I'd thought Jack and I might hike over to St Ives and pick up some fresh catch from the fishing boats. I was going to do one of my stews. But if you want to cook –

FRIEDA: (*Looking up.*) Yes, what a good idea! With the carrots and the fennel from the garden – how he does the carrots, butter-soft! He made it once for –

LAWRENCE: Frieda, write the bloody names.

FRIEDA: Oh, can't I speak at all now?

KATHERINE: Well, on Saturday, then, Jack and I can cook. Right, Jag?

JACK: What's that? There, finished!

LAWRENCE: Good man, sling 'em in. Come on, Frieda, it's not Einstein's General Relativity. Just put all my old girlfriends and your cousins like you always do.

FRIEDA: 'All' his girlfriends, I like that. All two?

JACK: Say, Frieda, is this fellow they call the Red Baron related to you?

FRIEDA: Yes, he is my cousin.

KATHERINE: What, the fighter pilot?

FRIEDA: Yes, Manfred von Richthofen.

KATHERINE: Not he of the gleaming teeth?

JACK: Gleaming teeth?

FRIEDA: No, another cousin, him I never met, he is from Poland, we're just distantly connected. But you can imagine how it makes me popular in Zennor when my cousin tells the newspapers he means to have a silver cup engraved with every English aircraft he shoots down.

JACK: They can't know he's your cousin, can they?

FRIEDA: You would be surprised, Jack, what they can know.

LAWRENCE: Are we ready, or is there a hell of a lot more to discuss?

FRIEDA: (*Hurling her papers in the hat.*) There, Mr High-and-Mighty!

LAWRENCE: About bloody time. Right, Mansfield, we'll start. You pick the pieces. Murry, got a watch?

JACK holds it up.

JACK: Ready, Tig? Steady…go!

KATHERINE takes a piece of paper from the hat and unfolds it. She repeats this until her turn is over.

KATHERINE: All right, wrote *Dubliners* –

LAWRENCE: James Joyce!

KATHERINE: You detest him… Minister for War –

LAWRENCE: Lloyd George!

KATHERINE: Think it's one of your old girlfriends –

LAWRENCE: Louie Burrows –

KATHERINE: No, the other –

LAWRENCE: Jessie Chambers!

KATHERINE: French president.

LAWRENCE: Poincaré!

KATHERINE: My old schoolfriend –

LAWRENCE: Ida Baker!

KATHERINE: Artist, ear-trumpet –

LAWRENCE: Dorothy Brett!

She opens one and bursts out laughing.

Come on, come on!

JACK: Stop! Time up!

KATHERINE: (*To LAWRENCE.*) Sorry, darling.

FRIEDA: Who was it made you laugh?

LAWRENCE: She can't say, it has to go back in. How many did we get?

KATHERINE: (*Counting.*) Five – no, six.

LAWRENCE: Good work. Give me the watch, Jack.

FRIEDA: Do you *hear* from Ida, Katherine?

KATHERINE: She's with her father in Rhodesia.

FRIEDA: For good?

LAWRENCE: Come on, get on with it, your turn.

KATHERINE mouths at FRIEDA 'no'.

Fighting fit, Murry?

JACK: Never better.

LAWRENCE: On your marks, get set, go! Frieda, go!

FRIEDA: *Mein Gott!* I'm going!

She takes a piece of paper from the hat.

Again! Lorenzo hates him.

JACK: Lloyd George.

FRIEDA: Yes. 'The Tramp'.

JACK: Charlie Chaplin.

FRIEDA: Yes. Hideous, ugly woman who believes herself the grand hostess –

JACK: Ott –

FRIEDA: – because she lives at Garsington –

JACK: Ottoline Morrell.

FRIEDA: – and can be something of a bitch. Correct! A poet, wrote a lot of stupid piffle about skylarks –

LAWRENCE: *Stop*!

FRIEDA: But that was not a minute!

JACK: Shelley?

FRIEDA: Yes! It's Shelley!

JACK: Can we have that?

KATHERINE: Not if your time was up –

FRIEDA: It wasn't! That was not a minute! That was not –

LAWRENCE: (*Dangerously.*) 'A lot of stupid piffle about skylarks'?

Beat.

FRIEDA: Yes, so what?

LAWRENCE: That's how you'd describe the work of Percy Shelley?

FRIEDA: Yes. I think it *is* piffle, his poems. I can describe him how I like. Anyway, Jack knew who I meant, didn't you Jack?

JACK: The skylarks rather gave the game away.

FRIEDA: So there it is.

LAWRENCE: Well, I look forward to your treatment of the rest of them in there. 'Mediocre playwright, wrote that shit about the Prince of Denmark.'

KATHERINE: Lorenzo dear, I'm sure that Frieda didn't –

LAWRENCE: 'Talentless Dago, fucked up the Sistine Chapel Ceiling'.

FRIEDA: Ah but Katherine, you soon will learn that only *he* has got the right to an opinion, because he is such a little God Almighty and the rest of us are just mere worms that scuttle on the surface of the earth.

LAWRENCE: You're worse than a worm – you're a bug – a bloodsucking bug that's feeding off my life.

FRIEDA: That's right, that's right, a worthless bug who can't have an opinion to herself or like or dislike anything without your say –

LAWRENCE: Who are you to lecture us on poetry, what on earth do you know?

FRIEDA: I am an educated woman!

LAWRENCE: At least Ottoline knows what the hell she's saying when she opens her bloody mouth!

FRIEDA: Oh, now, now I see it! This is all because I insulted his beloved Lady Ottoline, because he likes so much to be her lapdog and creep beneath her dirty skirts and give her what her husband cannot –

LAWRENCE punches the hat and its contents out of her hands. Pieces of paper fly everywhere.

JACK: Now steady on –

LAWRENCE: Your mind's diseased, you filthy whore!

FRIEDA: Yes, when he has no money and no-one else to pet him and admire him and tell him he's a genius –

LAWRENCE: I'll give you a dab on the cheek to quiet you, dirty hussy!

FRIEDA: – even though the work is hated and rejected –

LAWRENCE: I'm warning you!

FRIEDA: – no, no, and he cannot take rejection, cannot even take the smallest criticism –

LAWRENCE: Shut your mouth, you bitch!

FRIEDA: – no, because he is not after all a *man*!

LAWRENCE smashes the wine bottle on the edge of the table.

LAWRENCE: I'll cut your bloody throat!

He leaps to his feet and chases her around the table.

FRIEDA: Now you see it! Now you see what he is really like!

As he gains ground she starts to scream. KATHERINE and JACK are frozen in horror.

Help me! Jack, save me! Save me!

JACK ineffectually attempts to intercede. FRIEDA runs out into the garden, pursued by LAWRENCE. Her screams are heard.

JACK: Should I – do you think we ought to –

KATHERINE: No. Let them kill each other. Quicker the better, I say.

A piercing scream from outside.

JACK: Good God!

KATHERINE: This is worse than Cholesbury. And Cholesbury was hell on earth. Remember when we left I said I'd never, ever live with them again?

JACK: Perhaps they're drunk –

KATHERINE: Are you drunk?

JACK: No, but –

KATHERINE: This is the way they are.

JACK: They're tired, they'll sleep it off and patch it up tomorrow.

KATHERINE: If you like.

JACK: He'll be dreadfully sorry if he hits her.

KATHERINE: Mark my words, Jag. This is the beginning.

They stand in silence, listening. FRIEDA suddenly bursts back into the room, clutching her head and howling. LAWRENCE comes after her. He is holding a clump of her hair.

LAWRENCE: Come back here, you bitch! I'm not yet done with you!

FRIEDA: But I am done with *you!* I am done with *you!*

He catches up with her and thumps her. JACK attempts to stop him.

JACK: Lorenzo, stop it, it's gone far enough!

LAWRENCE: Let go of me, Murry!

JACK: But think what you're doing! Think!

Beat. LAWRENCE releases her and drops into the nearest chair, gasping for breath. FRIEDA stumbles, sobbing, to another chair. KATHERINE and JACK stare mutely at the table. Silence.

LAWRENCE sees a bit of paper on the floor. He picks it up, unfolds it. Finally, to JACK:

LAWRENCE: All right, easy one.

JACK: Beg your pardon?

LAWRENCE: Giant of French literature, addicted to coffee.

JACK stares at him, then glances at KATHERINE.

Good God, man, don't look at *her*! It's easy! Wrote through
the night, lived in terrible debt, drank gallons and gallons
of black –

JACK: B-Balzac.

LAWRENCE: *Thank* you.

JACK: You're welcome.

LAWRENCE: Christ's sake, you put the bastard *in*.

JACK: Yes, so I did.

Beat.

KATHERINE: Would anyone *like* some coffee?

JACK: Yes, that's a good idea. I'll make some, shall I?

KATHERINE: I'll do it.

*She exits swiftly into the kitchen. Silence. LAWRENCE and FRIEDA
stare at the floor. JACK blows his nose, needlessly. More silence.*

JACK: (*Desperately.*) Talking of Balzac.

No-one looks up.

I read the other day that when he, Balzac, was writing, he
began to believe in his characters so profoundly that he
actually thought they existed. So, one day, he's sitting at
home writing *Eugenie Grandet*, and a friend drops in and
starts telling him about his sister, the friend's sister, who's
seriously ill. And after a while Balzac thumps the table
and says, 'yes, yes, my dear fellow, that's all very well,
but more to the point, who the hell will we find to marry
Eugenie Grandet?

Beat.

LAWRENCE: That true?

JACK: Apparently!

Silence descends again.

FRIEDA: Always, Jack, when I think of Balzac –

JACK: (*Attentive.*) Yes?

FRIEDA: I remember that funny little place in Montparnasse, *Le Café Balzac.* Did you ever go there?

JACK: No, I don't believe I did.

FRIEDA: Oh, it was a typical artist place, full of course with poets, playwrights, journalists who never wrote a word but sat all day and drank and smoked and talked. The coffee was so strong it made you drunk almost. They had a parrot on the counter that said dirty things in French. And they had not got a menu – they had just one dish – but it was famous all through Paris –

LAWRENCE: (*In a terrible low voice.*) Macaroni Cheese.

FRIEDA looks up. They stare deep into each other's eyes. JACK glances from one to the other, gobsmacked.

FRIEDA: (*Softly.*) Do you remember?

LAWRENCE: How could I forget?

FRIEDA: How good it was, how tasty –

LAWRENCE: Very rich, but very good –

FRIEDA: Oh, very rich, extravagant, I think they put in cream –

LAWRENCE: And eggs, perhaps –

FRIEDA: And butter, melted butter –

LAWRENCE: Yes, and lots of kinds of cheese –

FRIEDA: Yes, Cheddar and gruyere and grated parmesan on top –

LAWRENCE: All crispy on the top –

FRIEDA: A little burnt –

LAWRENCE: A little caramelised –

FRIEDA: So good to eat!

LAWRENCE: So good!

FRIEDA: So really excellent!

They are smiling at each other.

LAWRENCE: Who else is like the macaroni cheese? All hard and crunchy on the top but underneath, so rich, so warm, so creamy –

FRIEDA: I don't know!

LAWRENCE: Who can it be?

FRIEDA: Give me a clue.

LAWRENCE: Oh, it's a clue she wants, all right…

He crosses the room and leans over her, whispering in her ear. She giggles and clutches at his back. They kiss with increasing urgency, almost sliding to the floor. JACK, mortified, gets down on his hands and knees and starts collecting the scattered bits of paper and putting them back in the hat. KATHERINE enters with a pot of coffee. She halts, incredulous.

End of Act One.

Act Two

SCENE ONE

Outside the cottages. Early afternoon, early June. A cool cloudy day. JACK kneels on the grass, painting the kitchen chairs with black paint. LAWRENCE is digging. He holds up a huge carrot.

LAWRENCE: Look at this, for instance.

JACK: All right.

LAWRENCE: *Look* at it! What is it?

JACK: It's a carrot.

LAWRENCE: But what else?

KATHERINE leans from the Tower window.

JACK: What do you mean, what else?

LAWRENCE: Great Scott, man! Look at it!

JACK: (*Trying.*) Well, it's –

LAWRENCE: Hell, Jack, have you've never looked inside your trousers?

JACK: Oh.

LAWRENCE: Well! You see that it's a phallic object?

KATHERINE: (*Calling.*) Lorenzo, you think *everything's* a phallic object. You ought to rename your cottage 'The Phallus' – why don't you?

LAWRENCE: Mansfield. How's the Muse?

KATHERINE: Dead, I think. And how appropriate: a funeral procession of chairs.

JACK stands back and squints at his handiwork.

71

JACK: Don't you like them? I think they look rather smart.

KATHERINE: Was there absolutely no other paint to be had?

JACK: None, I'm afraid.

KATHERINE: Well, we're going sit on them, not stare at them, so I don't suppose it really matters if they look like they belong in a waiting-room in Hades.

JACK: Oh dear. That bad?

KATHERINE: Just ignore me. Everything's that bad today.

LAWRENCE: I think misery improves her, don't you, Jack?

KATHERINE: Is that a compliment?

LAWRENCE: I can't decide.

JACK: Lorenzo's right, why don't you come and join us?

KATHERINE: Because I'm afraid I shall never see phallic objects in trees, in the running brooks, in stones and in everything, so I shan't be much use to you. Anyway, I have to just *get on.*

KATHERINE withdraws.

LAWRENCE: The point is, Jack, whether we're speaking of nature or art, the truth is that since the beginning of time the mystery of the phallic object has been –

Suddenly, FRIEDA appears, highly agitated, carrying a bag of shopping.

FRIEDA: Out of nowhere, they came! Out of nowhere! Hiding behind the wall, they were, crouching like animals, lying in wait!

LAWRENCE: What? Who were? What's happened?

FRIEDA: They leaped out at me, Lorenzo! They leaped out and I thought my heart would burst!

LAWRENCE grips FRIEDA by her upper arms.

LAWRENCE: Who leaped out at you, woman? Who?

FRIEDA: Coastwatchers! Two hateful coastwatchers lying in the grass like snakes!

LAWRENCE: What did they want?

JACK: Did they harm you?

FRIEDA: No, but they frightened me almost to death! I feel quite faint!

JACK: I'll fetch a glass of water, shall I?

FRIEDA: Yes – no – brandy, bring some brandy for the shock!

JACK: Brandy, right away.

He goes indoors.

LAWRENCE: Where were you?

FRIEDA: I was on the path from Zennor to St Just. I was just walking on the path and suddenly they leaped, they leaped from nowhere! And they knew my name!

LAWRENCE: Did you recognise them?

FRIEDA: One of them, the tall one, came here once before, with our policeman –

LAWRENCE: Sandy fellow, never said a word?

FRIEDA: Well, this time he said a word, this time he did!

LAWRENCE: What did he say?

JACK returns with a glass of brandy, which he gives to FRIEDA.

JACK: Here, drink this.

FRIEDA: How kind you are!

JACK: Just sip it slowly.

LAWRENCE: Go on then, what did he say?

FRIEDA drinks it all in one go. They wait. At last:

FRIEDA: 'Open that bag', he said. Just like that, so cold and hateful. 'Open that bag. We have reason to believe that you are carrying a camera.'

JACK: A camera?

FRIEDA: Oh, Jack, it was so horrible, so shaming. A group of girls from Zennor came along the path and stood and stared like they were in the stalls at Drury Lane.

LAWRENCE: So what did you do?

FRIEDA: (*Holding out her glass.*) A little more, please...my poor heart...

JACK fills it. She knocks it back.

So I thought, very well, then, if they want a show. So I said, 'oh, yes, Mr Coastwatcher, how right you are! I am carrying a camera!'

JACK: You didn't!

FRIEDA: But I did!

JACK: Magnificent!

FRIEDA: (*Starting to enjoy herself now.*) 'Yes,' I said, 'I am carrying a beautiful Kodak Brownie camera, would you like to look? It has been so very useful for me, as an émigré from Germany to be able to take such very wonderful photographs of your cliffs and coastline and send them to my old schoolfriends in the U-boats, and my cousin Manfred the Red Baron in his little fighter plane. Oh no, I would not be without my camera, one simply cannot be a proper spy without one!'

JACK: Gosh, Frieda, did you really say that?

FRIEDA: They could not believe it! They were as shocked as you!

JACK: What did they say?

FRIEDA: 'That's enough of your cheek, my lady,' says the other man, 'now open that bag this moment.' So –

FRIEDA takes the bag and pulls out a square block wrapped in white paper, which she upholds with a triumphant flourish.

JACK: A block of salt?

FRIEDA: 'So there's your camera!' I say to him. 'Three pennies worth of salt from Katie Berryman's shop! Would you like to try it? See how good a photograph you can take with that!' How I wish you could have seen it, Jack, I wish you could have seen their faces!

JACK laughs, but LAWRENCE has drawn apart, his face tightening with apprehension.

JACK: What a triumph! They must have been thoroughly mortified.

FRIEDA: They were! They were!

JACK: Did they apologise?

FRIEDA: Oh, 'Sorry to have troubled you, Frau Lawrence.'

LAWRENCE: (*Intensely.*) Did they actually say 'Frau'?

FRIEDA: 'You'll understand we only are doing our job, Frau Lawrence.'

JACK: What sort of bloody job is that? Harassing innocent women on the moors –

LAWRENCE: Frieda, did they really call you 'Frau'?

FRIEDA: Oh, *I* don't know, they might have done, what does it matter? What difference does it make?

LAWRENCE: There *is* a difference. Something's changed. The way they talk to us, it used to be disguised as something softer and more slippery, but ever since these wretched sinkings started, there's a difference. More direct, more threatening. They're tightening the net. And now they *dare* to call you Frau –

FRIEDA: But I *am* a Frau!

LAWRENCE: That's by the by. They were making a point.

JACK: On the other hand, Lorenzo, might it not be the reverse? I mean a sort of deference – to be polite, like one would say 'Madame'.

LAWRENCE: And is it deferent to pounce on her from nowhere? To force her into opening up her bag, is that polite? That's the height of etiquette, is it, Jack?

FRIEDA: Oh, well, perhaps they didn't say it after all.

LAWRENCE: What?

FRIEDA: They said so many things!

LAWRENCE: Did they say it or didn't they?

FRIEDA: I don't know!

LAWRENCE: For Christ's sake, Frieda, you *must* –

FRIEDA: (*Screaming.*) But I don't, Lorenzo! I don't know! I cannot recall exactly all the words they used, I was terrified out of my mind! But now it's not enough for them to cross-examine me without you do it too?

LAWRENCE: Damn!

FRIEDA: My poor heart –

LAWRENCE: They're closing in on us.

FRIEDA: My heart is thumping –

LAWRENCE: But I tell you this: they will not drive me out of here.

FRIEDA: It's not to do with you! It was to *me* it happened!

LAWRENCE: They can't. I've made my place here. I won't go.

He starts to leave.

FRIEDA: Where are you going now?

LAWRENCE: See William Henry. Find out what the talk is.

He goes. KATHERINE appears at the window, unnoticed. FRIEDA helps herself to brandy.

FRIEDA: How can he *go* like that? How can he leave me?

JACK: He was probably just –

FRIEDA: Probably just nothing! Only showing me once more he does not care!

JACK: He does, he does care terribly. You mustn't think that.

FRIEDA: Cares about himself, not me. I just am the Hunwife, I just am a millstone on his neck –

JACK: No, Frieda, he adores you.

FRIEDA: Does he? Does he?

JACK: God, Lorenzo worships you. You know he does.

FRIEDA: I *don't* know – ach, my head –

JACK: Are you all right?

FRIEDA: My head is spinning, I am faint –

She starts to sit on one of the chairs.

JACK: Wait, Frieda, wait, the paint's not –

He moves to catch her and they are momentarily suspended in an awkward embrace.

– dry. The paint's not dry.

Beat. She touches his face.

FRIEDA: So English. Always so English, in your little cage of Englishness. Poor little Jack. If you were mine, *mein Gott,* I'd show you freedom.

JACK: Frieda –

He gently takes her hand from his face and puts it by her side. FRIEDA laughs.

FRIEDA: She is a lucky woman, Katherine. I hope she knows how lucky.

JACK looks up at the window, but KATHERINE has moved away.

Scene ends.

SCENE TWO

Early morning. KATHERINE sits in the half-light of her study, writing. Outside it is flat and grey, with wild gusts of wind.

LAWRENCE: (*Off, calling.*) Murry! You ready? I can't hang about all day!

KATHERINE doesn't move. JACK enters, buttoning his shirt. He leans across her to open the window.

JACK: Morning!

LAWRENCE: Not for long it won't be.

JACK: What's that?

LAWRENCE: Get a bloody shift on, if you're coming.

JACK: Five minutes.

LAWRENCE: Hurry up then.

JACK sits down to lace his boots.

JACK: (*Pleased.*) Are you writing, Tig?

KATHERINE: A letter.

JACK: Oh, to whom?

KATHERINE: Koteliansky.

JACK: Say hullo from me.

KATHERINE: Why don't you add a line.

JACK: Um, yes.

JACK glances apprehensively at the window. KATHERINE notices.

KATHERINE: Oh, please, only if you can spare the time.

JACK: No, no, I'd like to.

He leans over her shoulder, reads for a moment.

Um, I say, darling…

KATHERINE: What?

JACK: Isn't this a bit –

KATHERINE: A bit?

JACK: I don't know – disloyal.

KATHERINE: Why? It's all true, isn't it? And it's *funny.* When I put it into words the way they behave seems entertaining rather than appalling. And if I didn't write it down I should go mad, and then, my dear, you'd be the only sane one here.

JACK: But – but is this really how you feel?

KATHERINE: What?

JACK: (*Reading.*) 'I am very much alone here. It is not really a nice place. It is so full of huge stones. But it is so very temporary. It may all be over next month; in fact it will be. I don't belong to anybody here, in fact I have no being –' Tig, how can you –

KATHERINE: How can I what? It's true.

JACK: You torture me when you say things like that.

KATHERINE: I 'torture' you? Really, Jack, you are absurd.

JACK: But I can't bear to think you're so alone.

KATHERINE: I wouldn't be alone if I were writing. I'd have no need of anyone or anything at all, including you.

JACK: (*Stiffly.*) Well, perhaps today might be a breakthrough.

KATHERINE: Why? Because you say so in that patronising, pompous tone of voice?

JACK: I don't intend to patronise you.

KATHERINE: What makes it any different from any other day? The sky's grey, the wind is howling and you're going for a walk with Lawrence. Just like yesterday and the day before that and the day before that. Just like every day for the last two months. So give me one good reason why today –

JACK: I don't have reasons. I have faith in you.

KATHERINE: Please don't. Your everlasting faith is the last thing I want. How do you suppose it makes me feel to think I'm disappointing you as well?

JACK: You'll never disappoint me, Tig, whether you write or –

KATHERINE: I'm a writer! I *have* to write! And if I'm not a writer –

JACK: But you *are* –

KATHERINE: – then tell me, Jack, what am I?

JACK: You're a writer through-and-through!

KATHERINE: Then *why can't I write?*

Beat. She is shaking with rage and frustration.

I'm not a wife. I'm not a mother. Half the time I'm hardly sure I'm a woman at all –

JACK: Don't, Tig, don't.

KATHERINE: Don't *what?* Tell the truth?

Beat.

JACK: All artists go through times when it doesn't come so easily.

KATHERINE: You don't.

JACK: Well, I –

KATHERINE: No, you don't. It's simple for you. You just sit there like a good little boy and the thoughts come and you write them down. Isn't that right, Jack? 'Application is all?'

JACK: It's simple for me because I don't have your talent. My work is an entirely different thing. I couldn't ever hope to write like you, you have a *gift* –

KATHERINE: Well, I wish to God I didn't. I wish I hadn't any gift at all and then it couldn't matter less. And I could be like Frieda, and be content with making pot-pourri and reading penny novels without feeling every second, every minute, that my life's seeping away and *nothing's getting done* –

She has a coughing fit.

JACK: My darling, Tig, what can I do to help? There must be something I can do, Tig, I'll do anything.

She stops coughing. A moment.

KATHERINE: Don't go with him today.

JACK: What?

KATHERINE: Tell him you're not coming. He's in a frightful mood, he's better off alone. Why not stay here and work with me downstairs? Let's write together like we did in Bandol, at that silly little table with our knees pressed together for warmth, remember?

She touches his face, strokes his hair.

Stay with me today, darling. We'll light the fire and draw the curtains and shut out the world and just be cosy. We'll have oranges and coffee and those gorgeous cigarettes that Ida sent, and after lunch we'll curl up under the rug and read to each other. Just think of it, Jaggle, just us, like two children all alone in a big ship rocking about on the sea.

LAWRENCE: (*Off.*) Murry, I'm going, d'you hear!

KATHERINE: (*Softly.*) Tell him. All you have to do is tell him.

Beat. JACK stares at her, agonised. She smiles and opens the window for him.

JACK: Um, Lorenzo?

LAWRENCE: (*Off.*) What? Are you coming or not?

JACK: Look, why don't you head off…

LAWRENCE: (*Off.*) Head off?

Beat.

JACK: Yes…yes, and I'll catch you up on the path.

LAWRENCE: (*Off.*) All right, but hurry bloody up.

JACK: On my way.

A gate slams, off. KATHERINE and JACK look at each other.

I'm sorry, Tig. I promised him. It seems unfair to let him down.

KATHERINE: Every day. You spend every single day with him.

JACK: I don't –

KATHERINE: And the fact is I can't tell from your hangdog manner whether you go to get away from me or because you're too scared to say no.

JACK: Neither!

KATHERINE: Well, I think both. I think you're absolutely petrified of us both.

JACK: (*Angry.*) All right, Tig, if that's what you think – then – then –

She stares at him, willing him to lose his temper. He sighs. Gently:

Look, I'm going to have to dash or he'll cut off without me, and you know what I'm like with a compass and map.

KATHERINE: Then stay. Please.

Beat.

JACK: (*With unconvincing enthusiasm.*) D'you know, I think you're going to have a good day today. In spite of everything I somehow feel you will. And, I'll be home before you know it, and after supper, we'll sit down together, just the two of us and –

KATHERINE: Oh, why don't you just go, if you're going.

She turns away from him back to her desk. JACK looks at her back, about to speak, then thinks better of it and leaves, closing the door deliberately behind him. KATHERINE drops her head on to the desk.

Moments pass. Then a vigorous knocking is heard.

FRIEDA: Katerina! Katerina! Are you busy?

KATHERINE: (*Without raising her head.*) Very.

FRIEDA stomps in, with a bowl of yoghurt. KATHERINE wearily lifts her head. FRIEDA throws herself into a chair and eats the yoghurt as she talks.

FRIEDA: Ach, I am exhausted. See how red, my eyes? A terrible night, again, we had. My stomach is like this – (*She holds up her hand and clenches and unclenches it.*) – colitis, from my nerves, the strain, my tongue is white, look – and the doctor says to eat fermented yoghurt but it does no good. Are these your cigarettes?

KATHERINE pushes them towards her.

And all because I dared to speak about my children. Because I dared offend the master of the universe by mentioning my little Barbara. And then he's off, a ranting raving lunatic, and you should hear the names he calls, the beasts I am compared with – worm, slug, bug, bitch, leech, snake, skunk -- and that's not all – apparently I also am a German sausage, great fat ham, a seeping lump of lard. Have you a match?

KATHERINE hands her a box of matches. She lights her cigarette, inhales it greedily.

Then he says, I make him sick, I nauseate him, I am death itself. 'You are a sickness in my lungs,' he says, 'you are a tumour growing on my soul.' Oh, Katherine, if you could hear the things he says!

KATHERINE: I usually can.

FRIEDA: But I will only take so much. 'This time,' I said, 'I'm leaving you. This time I have to go before you kill me. I will go to save myself.'

To KATHERINE's distaste, FRIEDA is now using the unfinished bowl of yoghurt as an ashtray.

Well, don't you want to know what he said?

KATHERINE: Would you like an ashtray?

FRIEDA: What? No, I have this. He said, 'Good! Go on', he said, 'good riddance!'. But he was afraid, I saw, his eyes were darting like a frightened hare's. Do you know why? Can you say why?

KATHERINE: (*Wearily.*) No, Frieda, why?

FRIEDA: Because he knows that he'd be nothing if I did. He'd be a paper bag, an empty tin without me *and he knows it*. And this always is the one thing I have over him, the little final power I have. That we both know he cannot live a single day without me.

KATHERINE: (*Looking out of the window.*) It's going to rain.

FRIEDA: Oh yes, he was afraid, I saw it in his eyes. He tried to bluster but he hadn't got the spirit, I can tell – the fight went out of him, his face was almost green – and then I know that I have won, and after that no matter what he says –

KATHERINE turns suddenly.

KATHERINE: So where will you go?

FRIEDA: *(Thrown)* What?

KATHERINE: When you leave him?

FRIEDA: When –

KATHERINE: When you leave Lawrence. What will you do?

FRIEDA: But Katherine, you're joking.

KATHERINE: Not a bit of it. I'm deadly earnest.

FRIEDA: But you know I cannot –

KATHERINE: Why not? There's no earthly reason not to, if you want to. You can go anywhere you like. You're free.

FRIEDA: But where? I couldn't go to Germany –

KATHERINE: Then go to London.

FRIEDA: London?

KATHERINE: You've got all sorts of friends who would be glad to have you – and you'd see the children.

FRIEDA: But how can I see them?

KATHERINE: I'm not suggesting that you saunter into Ernest's house, hang up your hat and ring for tea and toast – but at least you could be near them.

FRIEDA: No, I cannot.

KATHERINE: Why?

FRIEDA: I cannot. It's not possible.

KATHERINE: But why?

FRIEDA: I have no money –

KATHERINE: Get a job.

FRIEDA: *Now* you are teasing me.

KATHERINE: Why? There's no shortage of war-work. Join the Red Cross, drive an ambulance, you'd look marvellous in the uniform. It would perk the wounded up, at any rate.

FRIEDA: Be serious!

KATHERINE: I *am* serious. I think you ought to do it. It's the only way to show him that you mean it.

Beat. FRIEDA wrestles with this thought.

FRIEDA: Could you leave Jack?

KATHERINE: Well, I did, didn't I?

FRIEDA: But you came back.

KATHERINE: There you are then. Shows it can be done.

FRIEDA: But I don't think that you would leave him now. You would be mad to leave him.

KATHERINE lights a cigarette for herself. She stares at the climbing smoke through narrowed eyes.

KATHERINE: Oh, I often think I'd like to go away from everyone. I'd like to be completely and utterly alone.

FRIEDA: (*Shudders.*) No, I'd hate that. But you wouldn't like it really?

KATHERINE: I'd adore it. I'm only ever really happy on my own.

FRIEDA: What would you do?

KATHERINE: I'd drift about, and sit in parks and cafes, and live for all the little things that make me laugh, without having to explain myself to stupid people who aren't ever going to understand.

FRIEDA: But it's different for a woman like you –

KATHERINE: What do you mean, like me?

FRIEDA: Oh, you know what I mean.

KATHERINE: In fact, I don't.

FRIEDA: Who has her work, whose work come first! But me, I cannot even think of it. I am warm-blooded, I need warmth and love. I cannot even dream to go alone and leave my husband –

KATHERINE: Why? You left your children all right.

FRIEDA flinches. Beat.

Oh God, that was a hateful thing to say. I'm sorry.

FRIEDA: (*Crumpling.*) How can you say this, Katherine? How can you be so cruel? My children, my babies! Nobody will ever understand! Nobody!

FRIEDA puts her face in her hands and weeps loudly. KATHERINE touches her shoulder.

KATHERINE: Come on, Frieda, dear, don't cry. I didn't mean it. Let's go down and make some tea and just forget about it all.

FRIEDA doesn't budge. The drumming of rain is heard. After a moment, KATHERINE holds out her hand. Drops fall into her palm.

Frieda.

FRIEDA: (*Muffled.*) What?

KATHERINE: Frieda, it's raining.

FRIEDA: (*Muffled.*) Well, so what? What if it is? Why should I care?

KATHERINE: I mean, in the house. It's raining in the house.

FRIEDA looks up. Rain splashes through the roof.

Scene ends.

SCENE THREE

The Tower Cottage. Pots and pans of rainwater stand around. The fire is lit. LAWRENCE stands, in his dressing-gown, wet-haired, staring ruminatively into the fire. JACK enters, fully clothed but wet-haired, with a plate of sandwiches.

JACK: They're crab-paste. I'm afraid it's all we had. Here, have a glass of whiskey, warm you up. I hope you don't catch cold, Lorenzo, you were up on that roof for a jolly long time.

Beat. He glances up at the ceiling.

Seems like it's holding, anyway. If it holds until tomorrow then at least the girls'll know we made the effort. What time do you suppose their train comes in? Hey, we might borrow William Henry's cart and meet them at St Ives, mightn't we? Lorenzo?

LAWRENCE: We might and we might not.

JACK: I wonder who they've seen at Garsington.

LAWRENCE: Do you really, Jack?

JACK: At any rate, it feels as though they've been away for bloody ages.

Beat.

LAWRENCE: D'you ever feel like hitting something?

JACK: What?

LAWRENCE: I mean, someone. Hitting someone. Not a woman.

JACK: Um –

LAWRENCE: It's what some fellows do, when they feel bloody. They go in for some boxing or wrestling. Ju-jitsu, that sort of thing. There's a lot to be said for it.

JACK: Is there? Yes, I daresay there is. I've never really been the wrestling type, but I can quite imagine –

LAWRENCE: Why imagine? Why not do it? What's the worth in saying one's this type or that type? It only means that one rejects entire ways of being, cuts out whole swathes of experience that might have been infinitely valuable.

JACK: But by our age, one knows one's strengths, that's all. I'm good at Latin, I can write half-decent poetry when I'm in the mood –

LAWRENCE: But did you ever try it?

JACK: Wrestling? Not really.

LAWRENCE: Not really? Then you have a bit?

JACK: No. No, I haven't.

LAWRENCE: Then how do you know? You don't. Besides, it couldn't matter less about being the type, or being good at it, when it's between friends.

JACK: I suppose not. But equally one might have a friendly game of chess, or cribbage, and not risk breaking one's neck.

LAWRENCE: And not risk anything at all, eh? That's the way to live!

JACK: No, I don't mean –

LAWRENCE: No, you're right, Jack, that's the way to live. Risk nothing, do nothing, go nowhere. Keep your precious neck perfectly safe and play cribbage till you die at the table.

Beat.

JACK: Have *you* ever done it – wrestled – then?

LAWRENCE: Once. A fellow in Nottingham taught me.

JACK: And did you like it?

LAWRENCE: I don't know if I like it but I think it makes one sane. And I need to be sane, Jack, by God, I need to be sane. She's driven me to madness.

JACK: Frieda?

LAWRENCE: You don't know what it's like to live with her as I do. She's all-devouring, monstrous, suffocating. She's the great annihilator. And I can't go on. She's broken my spirit. I'm finished, Jack. I'm spent.

JACK: But Lorenzo, you can't let her do this to you. You can't let her destroy you like this.

LAWRENCE: I can't help it. I can't fight her anymore. She's killed me.

JACK: (*Distressed.*) It isn't true – it's just your state of mind.

LAWRENCE: My 'state of mind' is madness. I've gone mad.

JACK: And you think it would help you – to wrestle?

LAWRENCE: Yes!

He comes over to JACK, his tone eager, softer now.

I think it's important to wrestle and strive and be physically close. It keeps one sane and healthy. It makes a wholeness. For instance, you and I, we're mentally and spiritually intimate; we wrestle and strive on a cerebral plane – don't you agree?

JACK: Why, yes.

LAWRENCE: Then don't you think we should be physically intimate too? Otherwise there's this – incompleteness, this sense of not being whole. Don't you feel that?

JACK: (*Thoughtfully.*) I suppose I feel sometimes – a deep affection for you – and I don't know quite how to express it.

LAWRENCE: That's just it. Exactly. If we fight, we can express it.

JACK: But fighting is an opposition. An antagonism.

LAWRENCE: Or – a dance.

JACK: (*Hopefully.*) We can *dance*, if you like.

LAWRENCE: (*Smiling.*) Don't be so bloody soft. It's the fight I need.

Beat. LAWRENCE sighs deeply and returns his brooding gaze to the fire.

JACK: Would it be the *Blutbruderschaft* you wanted?

LAWRENCE: What?

JACK: If we – if we fought?

LAWRENCE: *Blutbruderschaft*…Yes, in a way.

JACK: Well – all right then.

LAWRENCE: Aha! Good man! Take off your clothes!

Suddenly animated, he throws off his dressing gown.

JACK: What?

LAWRENCE: Yes, it's better to be naked.

JACK: No, I don't think –

LAWRENCE: Good God, you're squeamish. Underclothes then.

JACK: Must we really?

LAWRENCE: Come on, get them off!

LAWRENCE heartily eats a few sandwiches and takes a swig of whiskey as JACK removes his clothes down to his undergarments.

LAWRENCE: Here, I'll show you some of the moves this fellow taught me. You must let me take hold of you like this –

JACK: Righto…

LAWRENCE: And then like this – and this –

He starts to wrestle JACK to the ground. Neither man is particularly fit, but LAWRENCE has an almost superhuman strength and becomes quickly absorbed in the fight. JACK is tossed hither and thither like a doll.

LAWRENCE: Come on, man, fight me! You're not fighting! Fight me!

JACK: Good God, Lorenzo, steady on –

LAWRENCE: Fight back! There's no resistance! Put some force behind it!

JACK: Sorry –

LAWRENCE: Don't apologise, for Christ's sake, show some spirit!

He lunges at JACK, grabbing him in a fierce headlock.

JACK: Ouch – stop – you're hurting me!

LAWRENCE: There, that's more like it, fight me!

JACK: Stop it! (*Choking.*) Let me go!

LAWRENCE: Then fight me, damn you! Fight me! Fight me! Fight me!

JACK punches him, hard, in the face.

Scene ends.

SCENE FOUR

The Tower Cottage. KATHERINE is serving tea to JACK, FRIEDA and LAWRENCE, who has a black eye, and is knitting ferociously. FRIEDA is eating a huge piece of cake. KATHERINE's mood is bright, hard, ebullient.

KATHERINE: So. Brett and Carrington send love, as does Kot, of course, who says London is quite deadly without us and he spends half his time praying for a Zeppelin to break the tedium. Gertler was supposed to come to Garsington yesterday but he spent so long at Paddington deciding which train to take that we couldn't wait and left before he got there.

FRIEDA: He will be furious! He thought that Katherine was proposing him some sort of assignation –

KATHERINE: Silly boy, he's such a fool. Meanwhile the house is full to bursting and the gardens are simply swarming with conscientious objectors – Ottoline's in her element, of course. Do you want cake, Lorenzo?

LAWRENCE: No.

KATHERINE: Just tea then?

LAWRENCE: Nothing.

KATHERINE: (*Softly.*) Suit yourself. Jack?

JACK: Thanks, Tig.

FRIEDA: (*Mouth full.*) Tell them about when we first arrived –

KATHERINE: What?

FRIEDA: (*Swallowing.*) About when we first arrived –

KATHERINE: That's right, as we came up the drive, Clive Bell was sitting in a pear-tree on the lawn –

LAWRENCE: Oh, for fuck's sake, *shut up.*

A shocked beat.

FRIEDA: *Lorenzo* –

LAWRENCE: Do you think I want to hear about these people? Sitting in pear trees and praying for air-raids for entertainment, sipping good champagne and playing parlour games while a generation blazes to death? Christ, it's only when one's properly away from that sort that one sees how revolting and degraded and perverse they really are.

KATHERINE: Clive and the others are conscientious objectors, Lawrence. Like you.

JACK: (*Warningly.*) Tig.

LAWRENCE: They're not conscientious objectors! They don't have a conscience, not a single one of 'em. They object to nothing but the thought of being sent to filthy trenches with rude, uncouth men – men like me, and getting their fingernails chipped, and maybe, if the Germans aren't aware of proper British class distinctions, getting blown to little bits. They don't object to *war*! They love it! They adore it! This war's the grand excuse they've always wanted, the perfect reason for them just to loaf about doing nothing, nothing at all –

KATHERINE: But what are *we* doing? Here? What are we doing?

LAWRENCE thumps the table.

LAWRENCE: If you don't see the difference, Mansfield, there's no hope for you! You've gone wrong, you know, badly wrong, you've gone wrong to your core, you've gone wrong in your sex –

KATHERINE: Oh, back to that, are we?

LAWRENCE: You belong to an obscene spirit!

KATHERINE: Then I wish he'd come and take me away!

FRIEDA: Stop it, you two!

Beat. They stare at each other, smoldering.

Come, let's talk of something else. Who wants more cake?

KATHERINE: All right. Perhaps Lawrence would like to tell us how he really got that nasty shiner.

JACK: Tig –

KATHERINE: Because quite frankly, the tale of falling from the Tower roof –

LAWRENCE gets up and exits.

– I didn't find entirely convincing.

The door slams behind LAWRENCE. Beat.

FRIEDA: Oh dear. Oh dear, I had better go to him.

JACK: Yes, better had.

FRIEDA: I'll just have this.

She ploughs her way through her cake. They watch her silently. At last she finishes.

I'll go to him, that's best. I'll go to him.

She hurries after LAWRENCE.

KATHERINE starts to clear the table. After a while:

KATHERINE: Well?

JACK: What?

Beat.

It wasn't much. He wanted us to wrestle and I –

KATHERINE: Wanted you to *wrestle*?

JACK: He explained it to me and it seemed to make such sense, the way he put it. But he was raging like a bull. He badly wanted to hurt me – and he wanted me to hurt him. And although he's by far the stronger there were moments when I could have, yes, I could have hurt him, but I didn't

96

want to. Only he pushed and pushed until at last I lost control and walloped him completely. Tig, are you all right?

She has turned away.

You're not – you're not *laughing,* are you, Tig?

KATHERINE: I'm sorry. I'm sorry, but it's all too absurd.

She puts her face in her hands. She is laughing helplessly.

JACK: But it isn't funny. Lorenzo's hurt – I mean he's truly hurt, not just his eye. I think he honestly believes I've let him down – but in some grievous way that means much more than just not wanting to wrestle with him –

KATHERINE: (*Laughing.*) Oh, Jag, stop it, do! If you had the least idea what you sound like!

JACK: He barely spoke to me after that. Something altered in that moment, Tig, something shifted. I felt the air between us change.

KATHERINE: It's him who's changed. He's quite unrecognisable.

JACK: It's *her,* though. It's because he's so dashed miserable with *her.* She almost tortured him to death before we came, you know. We don't see the half of it, Tig, she's a perfectly monstrous woman –

KATHERINE: Oh, you don't have to persuade *me!* I've just spent four unbroken days with her. She's frightful – false – demented. You ought to have seen her at Garsington, how she was everyone's best friend until they went to powder their nose. I can quite believe she's capable of anything.

JACK: And she's so much tougher than he is. He's quite lost, you know.

KATHERINE: Lost like a little gold ring in an enormous German Christmas pudding. And with all the appetite in the world, I'm afraid one can't eat one's way through Frieda to find him.

JACK: God, why won't someone cut her into bits so he'd see the light again?

KATHERINE: He doesn't want to see the light.

JACK: Poor Lorenzo, it's too terrible for words.

KATHERINE: Except it isn't, really, is it? The war's 'terrible'. This frightful fighting in Jutland. My little brother blown to bits for no reason, for a country that's not even *his*, in a war that hasn't a thing to do with him – *that's* 'terrible'. But really, Jack, all it takes is a day or two away from this lunatic asylum to realise what nonsense it is. What utterly laughable nonsense.

JACK: What do you mean? What's nonsense?

KATHERINE: All of it. The 'community'. *Rananim.* Us. Them. The whole lot of it.

Beat.

I've had more addresses than birthdays.

JACK: What?

KATHERINE: It's true. I worked it out on the train, whilst Frieda was sitting in a nest of newspapers sucking lemon drops and banging on about the price of pig iron. I smiled and nodded and looked fascinated, and in my head I worked out: I've had twenty-nine addresses since I left New Zealand.

JACK: Twenty-nine?

KATHERINE: Since you and I have been together, we've moved sixteen times.

JACK: Have we really?

KATHERINE: And six of those moves have been to do with Lawrence.

Beat.

JACK: What are you saying?

KATHERINE: Nothing's holding us, that's all. We're free.

JACK: You're not suggesting –

KATHERINE: We don't have to live like this.

JACK: What, *leave*?

KATHERINE: *I hate it, Jack!* I hate everything about it. I hate the cold and the damp and the flat land and the wind that tears your skin and the cruel sea and the huge stones; the whole place is a giant graveyard. Nothing grows here, nothing flowers – and nor can I. I can't write here, I can't live here. And whether you come with me or not –

JACK: Tig!

KATHERINE: If we stay here, Jack, it's going be the end of us. So either we leave here together, soon, or this is it. We go our separate ways.

Beat.

JACK: Where would we go?

KATHERINE: William Henry's mother says that Mylor on the south coast is so much more mild and sunny –

JACK: Don't tell me you've spoken of this to Mrs Hocking?

KATHERINE: She got on the train at Plymouth, she'd been to see her sister.

JACK: But Frieda –

KATHERINE: Oh, Frieda was gorging herself in the buffet-car for the hundredth time.

JACK: But what if Mrs Hocking says something to William Henry?

KATHERINE: Well, what if she does? We need advice, if we're to stay in Cornwall.

JACK: But Lorenzo – he mustn't find out!

KATHERINE: But –

JACK: No, he can't, Tig, he can't – he can't ever find out!

Beat.

KATHERINE: Tell me, Jack. What is it that you're so afraid he'll do to you? Try to stab you with his grouting knife again, or wrestle you to death?

JACK: Don't, Tig.

KATHERINE: But what on earth are you so frightened of? I know he's full of wind and fury but my God, he's just a man! He's just a man like you!

JACK murmurs something unintelligible.

What? I can't hear you.

JACK: I said –

He can't look at her.

KATHERINE: (*Gently.*) What, my love? What is it, Jaggle? Tell me.

JACK: He may not be my friend anymore.

She stares at him helplessly.

Scene ends.

SCENE FIVE

Mermaid Cottage. LAWRENCE sits in his pyjamas, writing feverishly. He looks white and haggard. There is a pot of coffee on the table beside him. He pours out another cup, takes a sip and returns to writing.

FRIEDA comes slowly down the stairs in her nightgown.

FRIEDA: How can you work in this darkness? You'll spoil your eyes.

She opens the curtains and stands there a moment.

Do you think that it will ever stop raining? How can there be such water in the skies? It is July! It should be sun and strawberries and picnics at the cove. Not umbrellas and galoshes and…

Beat.

You didn't come to bed again.

LAWRENCE: No.

FRIEDA: Why?

LAWRENCE: I was writing.

FRIEDA: All night?

LAWRENCE: I'm a writer.

FRIEDA: And the night before?

LAWRENCE: Yes, probably.

FRIEDA: Nobody writes all day and all the night.

LAWRENCE: Don't tell me any writer wouldn't, if he could.

FRIEDA: Oh-ho! Someone is pleased with himself!

LAWRENCE: Aye. P'raps I am. Why shouldn't I be? What's wrong with being confident in what one does? I can do it. If I choose, I can do it all night.

FRIEDA: What a man.

LAWRENCE: And besides, I can't sleep. There's no point going to bed. My mind's on fire.

FRIEDA: Time was, you came to bed for *me*.

LAWRENCE: Frieda –

FRIEDA: Oh, it doesn't matter about that, but if you had some fresh air you might sleep. For weeks you've hardly stepped outside the door. You hardly eat, you hardly shave or wash –

LAWRENCE: *Because I have to write this!*

Beat.

It's in my head. All the time. Every minute. Real and fresh and urgent and alive. A living world of living characters who grow and change and clamour and demand to be acknowledged. I am responsible to them and them alone. I can't stop now. Don't ask me to.

FRIEDA: I only meant you ought to wash your teeth from time to time…

LAWRENCE: And of course no-one'll want to publish it, and if it does get published I expect they'll flagellate me for it, but I don't give a damn about that. It's going to be good, this book – and it's going to be what I intended.

FRIEDA: (*Flatly.*) Well, hurrah.

LAWRENCE: That's all you have to say?

FRIEDA: You're writing about *them,* aren't you.

Beat.

LAWRENCE: It's about two sets of couples, polarised. That doesn't mean –

FRIEDA: I am not a fool, Lorenzo. I know what it means. Not because we talk together openly about your writing anymore, but because the rare times when you do come up to bed – you talk about it in your sleep.

LAWRENCE: I don't –

FRIEDA: You do! You shout out words and sentences and sometimes whole entire paragraphs. And sometimes just one name, and I can promise you, it isn't mine. You shout his name, Lorenzo, in your sleep. And they must hear it through the walls as clear as I do lying next to you.

Beat.

LAWRENCE: Leave me alone.

FRIEDA: But what has he *done* to you, Lorenzo?

LAWRENCE: I've work to do, just leave me. Go away.

FRIEDA: Why will you not talk with him? Why don't you take your walks together anymore? They are next door and we are strangers! I am a prisoner here!

LAWRENCE: Why are *you* a prisoner? Go next door if you like. Go wherever the hell you want but leave me be.

FRIEDA: I only want to understand. What has he done? How did he so offend you? What is it that you ask of these men to be always disappointed? Is it love? Is it sex?

LAWRENCE: Christ Almighty.

FRIEDA: Is it connected somehow with your father –

LAWRENCE: No, it bloody isn't!

FRIEDA: Are you trying to resolve somehow your anger with your father through these male relationships that –

LAWRENCE: What in hell are you talking about?

FRIEDA: Sigmund Freud has said –

LAWRENCE: Fuck Sigmund Freud.

FRIEDA: I'd like to but I think he's in Vienna.

LAWRENCE laughs shortly. Beat.

Sex is different. Sex, I understand. But this. This building up, this elevating of a man and then his slow destruction. This I cannot understand.

LAWRENCE: It isn't like that.

FRIEDA: I could list them! I could list the men with whom you've done this!

LAWRENCE: You don't know anything about it.

FRIEDA: Yes I do, you've told me, fifty thousand times. How all these men betrayed you. Jessie Chambers' brother –

LAWRENCE: That was different –

FRIEDA: And George Neville also, then your friend McLeod, Arthur McLeod in Croydon, and I saw it all myself of course with Bunny Garnett! I saw it happening right there before my eyes!

LAWRENCE: Saw *what*?

FRIEDA: I don't know – this – whatever you want to call it! This friendship, whatever, this love –

LAWRENCE: (*Bellowing.*) Friendship *is* love!

FRIEDA: Then you expect too much from it.

LAWRENCE: *Expect* too much?

Beat. With immense suppressed emotion:

If I expect a lot then it's because I give myself completely. My whole self, completely. Everything I am. Because a friendship is as binding and as solemn as a marriage. It's a covenant for life. And when I say a man's my friend, I mean that I'll love him forever and keep faith with him as long as I live. And whatever that man asks of me, I will give with all my heart.

FRIEDA: And Jack?

LAWRENCE: What about him?

FRIEDA: Will you love him forever? Will you keep faith with him all through your life, no matter what?

LAWRENCE: If he can prove this friendship matters half as much to him –

FRIEDA: (*Softly.*) *Sie gehen weg.*

LAWRENCE: What?

FRIEDA: *Sie gehen weg,* Lorenzo. They're leaving.

Beat. He stares at her.

I heard them talking yesterday. They were on the lane behind the house and I was in the garden. They didn't see me – I crouched down behind the rhododendron. Funny, isn't it? At last I really am a German spy.

She laughs sadly.

Your friend Jack was apparently in Mylor at the weekend. He was looking for a cottage. I think from what they said, he must have found one.

LAWRENCE is very still. FRIEDA watches him fearfully.

Did I do wrong to tell you? I didn't want to but I could not keep it back a moment more. Oh Lorenzo. What will you do?

LAWRENCE: Do?

FRIEDA: What will you say to them?

Beat. LAWRENCE looks down at his papers. He suddenly looks up.

LAWRENCE: I'd be glad if you'd read some of this, you know.

FRIEDA: Lorenzo, have you understood one single word I've said?

LAWRENCE: (*Rifling through papers.*) The beginning isn't right yet – here, I'll give you some from chapter two. I want to know what you think before I go on. I want to know if the characters interest you, if it makes you want to know the rest.

FRIEDA: But Lorenzo –

LAWRENCE: Because your opinion matters to me more than anything on earth. I can't go on, you see – I can't go on without you.

Beat. She stares at him, bewildered.

FRIEDA: Now?

LAWRENCE: Yes, have a look at it now.

FRIEDA: Well, all right. If you really want me to.

LAWRENCE: Good lass.

She sits and starts to read. LAWRENCE paces.

FRIEDA: She asked us to supper tonight. What shall we do?

LAWRENCE: Are you reading this or not?

FRIEDA: I am, but still we have to tell her if we're coming.

Beat.

Well, what shall I tell her?

LAWRENCE: Tell her she can stick her –

FRIEDA: Please, Lorenzo!

LAWRENCE: I suppose you want to go.

FRIEDA: I don't know. I don't know. But maybe if we had a happy time – if we had fun again and laughed together – and were only kind and friendly to each other – then maybe, perhaps –

LAWRENCE: Do you really care so much?

FRIEDA: Don't you?

LAWRENCE: Not a damn. They can do as they please. I won't pander to a worm like Jack to make him change his mind. If they want to go, they ought to go.

FRIEDA: You don't mean that.

LAWRENCE: Tell you what, we ought to move in there! We could, at any rate, it's paid for till next year –

FRIEDA: But they haven't even said –

LAWRENCE: Perhaps they'll say tonight. Perhaps that's why they asked us.

FRIEDA: Oh, I do hope not, I do hope not!

LAWRENCE: It's the least they could do to be open and honest –

FRIEDA: Yes, but promise you'll say nothing, if we go. Say nothing, please, just please let it be nice.

LAWRENCE: All right, all right, I promise.

FRIEDA: Then we'll go, shall we, for supper?

LAWRENCE: If you like. We'll go. Now *read.*

FRIEDA sighs deeply, and returns her attention to the manuscript. She flips through the pages, glancing ahead.

FRIEDA: Is this what you're calling it? 'Women in Love'?

LAWRENCE: I think so. D'you like it?

FRIEDA: I don't know. I suppose so.

Beat.

Seems a funny title, when it's all about the men.

Scene ends.

SCENE SIX

The Tower Cottage. KATHERINE, JACK, FRIEDA and LAWRENCE sit around the table. They are playing the Hat Game. The mood is one of heightened jollity, an almost hysterical brightness.

FRIEDA: Played Hamlet, French actress, one leg –

KATHERINE: Sarah Bernhardt.

FRIEDA: Austrian psychoanalyst –

KATHERINE: Freud, Sigmund Freud.

FRIEDA: Wrote 'Keep The Home Fires Burning.'

KATHERINE: Ivor Nov –

JACK: Stop!

KATHERINE: Can we have him? Ivor Novello?

JACK: What d'you think, Lorenzo?

LAWRENCE: Well, it isn't strictly legal, but they might as well.

FRIEDA: Why, Katerina, we're superbly good tonight!

KATHERINE: How many?

FRIEDA: Nine!

JACK: Damn it, Lorenzo, they don't need our generosity.

LAWRENCE: Just wait, my lad, we'll catch 'em up by stealth. Who's for more wine?

He pours wine for everyone, singing:

> 'They were summoned from the hillside, they were called in from the glen,
> And the country found them ready at the stirring call for men
> Let no tears add to your hardship as the soldiers pass along
> And although your heart is breaking, make it sing this cheery song...'

All together now!

ALL: 'Keep the home fires burning
While your hearts are yearning
Though your lads are far away they dream of home.
There's a silver lining, through the dark clouds shining
Turn the dark cloud inside out, till the boys come home!'

All applaud and whistle.

FRIEDA: Oh, it *is* a jolly tune!

LAWRENCE: Oh, it *is*. Nothing like a jolly tune to put some sparkle in a bit of pugilistic propaganda! Speaking of which, I want to know, which one of you scoundrels will confess to putting Lloyd bloody George in the hat again?

FRIEDA: I did!

KATHERINE: I did too.

LAWRENCE: Murry?

JACK: Guilty as charged.

LAWRENCE: Are you?

JACK: What?

LAWRENCE: Well, I put him in too, so there's three more of the little Welsh bastards swimming about in there.

JACK: All right, here's a test. *Keep The Home Fires Burning* – who wrote the lyrics?

FRIEDA: Ivor Novello!

JACK: The *lyrics*. He wrote the music.

KATHERINE: Was it you, dear?

FRIEDA: It wasn't, was it, Jack? So modest –

LAWRENCE: 'Course it bloody wasn't! Go on, who?

JACK: It was an American poet, name of Lena Guilbert Ford.

FRIEDA: Who?

JACK: She and Novello were working together one night and he was struggling to find an image for the song. And then the maid came in and put another log on the fire, and the fire blazed up, and Novello shouted, 'that's it! That's exactly what I mean! The hearth, the home fires burning!' And Mrs Ford went off and wrote the lyrics in just under half an hour.

FRIEDA: And is it not typical, Katherine? The man shoots off to stardom and the woman in left standing in the shadows. Who has ever heard of Mrs Ford?

JACK: Only the horrid thing is, how d'you suppose *I* did?

KATHERINE: Tell us, Jag, is she the mother of your unborn child?

JACK: No, I read her obituary in *The Times*. She got killed in an air-raid in London last week.

FRIEDA: Oh, no!

LAWRENCE: Christ, Jack, what a heartwarming little vignette!

KATHERINE: He can always be relied on to get a party going, can't you darling.

JACK: Well, I thought it was interesting, that's all.

LAWRENCE: (*Playful, but with a certain steeliness.*) Poor old Murry. He's the only proper genius in the room, you see. If he finds something interesting, it's simply interesting. Raw emotion needn't interfere.

JACK: Now that's unfair!

LAWRENCE: Is it? Come on then, our turn. Going to time us, ladies?

FRIEDA: I will.

LAWRENCE: Righto. Ready, Jack?

JACK: I am.

LAWRENCE: (*Coolly.*) Excellent.

LAWRENCE draws his first piece of paper from the hat. Barely looking at it, he speaks calmly and unhurriedly.

British diplomat, charged with treason.

JACK: Sir Roger Casement.

LAWRENCE: American general, plotted to surrender West Point.

JACK: Benedict Arnold.

LAWRENCE: Mastermind of the Gunpowder Plot.

JACK: Guy Fawkes.

FRIEDA's expression is becoming apprehensive.

LAWRENCE: Betrayed his friend for thirty bits of –

JACK: Judas Iscariot.

FRIEDA: Stop!

LAWRENCE: Now, here's a good one.

FRIEDA: (*Wildly.*) Stop!

JACK: Is that it?

LAWRENCE: Wrote the soon-to-be-published *Fydor Dostoevsky; A Critical Study* –

JACK: Me.

FRIEDA: You promised, Lorenzo!

LAWRENCE: Born in Peckham, studied at Oxford –

KATHERINE: Promised what?

JACK: Jack Murry! Me!

LAWRENCE: Currently residing in Zennor, Cornwall –

JACK: Jack *Middleton* Murry?

LAWRENCE: And shortly to move south, to Mylor.

Beat. JACK and KATHERINE are frozen.

FRIEDA: Oh, Lorenzo…

LAWRENCE: What's the matter? Why so quiet? Why, anyone'd think the two of you had something to hide!

Looking at JACK, he sings softly.

'Overseas there came a pleading
"Help a nation in distress"
And we gave our glorious laddies, honour bade us do
  no less

For no gallant son of freedom to a tyrant's yoke should
bend
And a noble heart must answer to the sacred call of
"Friend".'

*On the last word, he flings the hat full of paper in JACK's face. A
moment.*

JACK: I wanted to tell you. I didn't know how.

LAWRENCE: Don't creep to me, worm. Don't crawl. I'm sick to
death of your crawling and your creeping. You sicken me,
Murry. You repulse me.

KATHERINE: Oh, stop it, Lawrence. It's not his fault. It's me
who wants to leave.

LAWRENCE: Don't worry, Mansfield. I'm well aware that
you're the poisonous one. He's a crawling worm, a sickly
leech that has gorged and grown fat on my life-blood, but
you. You're the snake in the grass. You're the serpent in
Eden.

KATHERINE: Good God, Lawrence, do you really think that
this is Eden? This isn't Eden! This is *Cornwall.*

LAWRENCE: Well, it was Eden once, before you blighted it.

KATHERINE: Then let us go! Just let us go, with grace.

Beat. LAWRENCE slumps a little. FRIEDA suddenly surges up.

FRIEDA: If you had only just been honest with us, Katherine!
This is what hurt us most, that you must lie and sneak
about behind our backs –

KATHERINE: Oh, shut up, Frieda.

LAWRENCE: Don't you speak to her like that!

KATHERINE: Forgive me, is it only you who gets to speak to
her like that? I suppose you've a monopoly on bugs and
snakes and leeches too –

LAWRENCE: There are no creatures foul enough for what you are. Bugs and leeches don't come close. An alley-cat's too good for you. Why, you couldn't even be faithful to *him* –

JACK: Don't, Lorenzo.

LAWRENCE: – what a fool I was to think you'd be faithful to us.

KATHERINE: You don't know anything about –

LAWRENCE: Only I do, you see, you nasty little slut.

JACK: Lorenzo, *don't.*

LAWRENCE: Nasty little, filthy little whore, crawling on your slimy belly to Dijon and making love to filthy Frenchmen. Tell us, Mansfield, how many officers did you screw to get into the war-zone?

KATHERINE: (*To JACK.*) Are you going to allow this?

JACK: (*To LAWRENCE.*) Look, I think you ought to go.

KATHERINE: (*To JACK.*) That's it, is it?

LAWRENCE: How many dirty secrets have you got behind that sanctimonious little mask you call a face? Why don't you let her out? Why don't you let the filthy little slut out, let her leave her trail of slime across the page. Who knows, you might even write something worth reading one day.

KATHERINE: Something that might get pilloried and suppressed and bang me up in court for writing smut? Or perhaps just something 'windy, tedious, boring and nauseating' –

LAWRENCE: That's it, little bitch! Let her out!

KATHERINE: You were right about that, by the way, it *is* rather hard to forget.

FRIEDA: (*Suddenly, hysterically.*) Stop it, both of you, shut up!

LAWRENCE: No, you'll never really let her out, you'll never tell the truth. You'll let it fester, the black disease of all the filthy secret things you've done. And I hope to God one day it kills you –

JACK: (*Very loudly.*) *DESIST! DESIST! DESIST!*

Everyone stops and looks at him. A beat.

FRIEDA: What did he say?

JACK: (*Quietly.*) I said 'desist'. I don't know why I chose that particular word.

LAWRENCE, looking at him, almost smiles. Then he suddenly turns and lurches out of the door.

FRIEDA: Lorenzo! Where is he going? Go after him, Jack.

KATHERINE: Oh, let him walk it off –

FRIEDA: And if he hurls himself into the sea! How would you live with that?

KATHERINE: Quite comfortably at this moment!

JACK: Look, I'll go.

KATHERINE: No, stay. I'll go.

KATHERINE exits after LAWRENCE. FRIEDA and JACK sit awkwardly at the table.

JACK: Mylor isn't even all that far away, you know. You can come and visit us, and we can visit you. It's really rather pretty, and there's room for –

FRIEDA: Would you do a favour for me, Jack.

JACK: Of course. Anything. What can I do?

FRIEDA: Don't talk.

JACK nods. They sit in silence.

115

LAWRENCE is standing on the patch of grass in front of the cottages, looking out to sea.

KATHERINE approaches quietly.

KATHERINE: You know, we shouldn't be enemies, you and I. We're the ones who really understand each other. Perhaps that's been the problem all along. We're the ones who should be friends.

Beat.

And I do know how it feels, to love so much you don't know where to *put* the love. To be so full of homeless, rootless, surplus love that hasn't anywhere to go. For what it's worth, I do know how that feels.

Beat.

One day I expect we'll look back on this as a rather nice holiday.

LAWRENCE: (*Tersely.*) Something's happening out there.

KATHERINE: What?

LAWRENCE: Look. The lights.

Slowly, voices are heard shouting, gathering volume. FRIEDA and JACK emerge from the house.

FRIEDA: What's happening, what's that noise?

KATHERINE: I don't know – look, the little lights, they're moving –

JACK: Lanterns. Those are lanterns. Going down towards the sea.

LAWRENCE: It's wreckers.

FRIEDA: What?

LAWRENCE: A ship's gone down. A U-boat must have got it. Those are wreckers swarming down like rats to make off with the pickings.

KATHERINE: How absolutely horrible.

LAWRENCE: Not really. It's survival.

They stand in silence, watching. Voices all around. And suddenly, an explosion. A red light filters through the sky.

JACK: My God, someone's set fire to it! It's burning up!

LAWRENCE: That's it! Incinerate the wreckers like bugs in a carpet!

FRIEDA: Don't say that, Lorenzo, I hope there are not people –

LAWRENCE: Would you look at that!

FRIEDA: I don't know why are you so happy when there might be people –

LAWRENCE: I'd call that pretty nearly an absolute symbol, wouldn't you, Murry?

JACK: What?

LAWRENCE: Isn't that what you'd call it, in the hallowed halls of literary criticism? Nothing better than a metaphor to cap a story, is there? Nothing better than a bloody symbol!

He grins delightedly at them all as the sky blazes around them.

Scene ends.

SCENE SEVEN

Day. KATHERINE stands in her study, packing her journal and her manuscript into her bag. She stops and surveys the room, empty apart from her hat, which still hangs on the wall. She lights a cigarette. Smokes.

JACK enters.

JACK: You ready, Tig?

KATHERINE: Queer thing, isn't it. With everything packed up, it's just a house. A house in which one has been so unhappy, and yet when it comes to leaving, all one can recall are the moments of….

> *Beat.*

JACK: William Henry said he'll take us to the station.

KATHERINE: Did he?

JACK: But we ought to hurry if we want to get the half-past twelve.

> *Beat.*

KATHERINE: (*Slowly.*) I'm not entirely sure we're going to make it, Jack.

JACK: It's only quarter-to!

KATHERINE: No, not the train.

JACK: Then what?

> *Beat.*

KATHERINE: Sometimes I wonder if you really do misunderstand me, or if it's just your way of making sure we never have a real conversation.

JACK: Well, I sincerely promise you, right now I haven't the ghost of an idea what you're talking about. All I know is that William Henry's waiting for us outside and I told the Mylor woman we'd collect the keys by half-past three –

KATHERINE: All right, all right. I'm ready.

She puts out her cigarette and gathers up her possessions, struggling to accommodate them all. She reaches for her hat.

JACK: Here – give me the bag.

KATHERINE: No, I can manage.

JACK: Let me bring your hat, then.

KATHERINE: Goodbye, Tower. Goodbye, Zennor.

Beat.

On we go.

KATHERINE exits. JACK takes her hat from the hook. He stands a moment, troubled, turning it in his hands. Then, with a sigh, he follows her.

Scene ends.

SCENE EIGHT

A warm, autumnal day, over a year later. It is October 1917. The door to Tower Cottage stands wide open and the room has been ransacked. Chairs and tables overturned, papers strewn over the floor. FRIEDA sits in the middle of it all, turning an envelope in her hands.

LAWRENCE appears in the doorway.

LAWRENCE: Christ, what's happened? Are you hurt?

He rushes over to her.

FRIEDA: (*Numb.*) Where were you?

LAWRENCE: I was in the fields with William Henry – helping with the harvest –

FRIEDA: I tried to find you. I went even to the farm but the men did not know where you'd gone.

LAWRENCE: Was it the coastguards? Tell me what they did.

FRIEDA: I sat and had a cup of tea with William Henry's mother, I didn't want to but she made me stay, she said that I look pale. She said I must come with you more often and not hide away. How kind she was –

LAWRENCE: Frieda, what happened?

FRIEDA: She asked me all about my children. I told everything. She said I must be lonely this last year since Katherine went. Yes, I said. I am. Lorenzo's never home these days. I always am alone, he's never there. Always with William Henry, always helping in the fields.

LAWRENCE: Look, I'm sorry, I'm sorry I left you, for God's sake, what happened?

FRIEDA: It's Katherine's birthday today. Did you know? October fourteenth. Koteliansky wrote and said they are in London now.

LAWRENCE: *Frieda*!

FRIEDA: I don't know! I don't know what happened! I came back from the farm and here it was. They must have come while I was out, they must have watched me leave –

LAWRENCE: Who, coastwatchers?

FRIEDA: Yes, I suppose, or the police, or both.

LAWRENCE: (*Slumps, defeated.*) Dear God.

FRIEDA: (*Weeping.*) Why are they doing this? Why, why do they hate us?

LAWRENCE: Whatever they're looking for, whatever they're hoping to find, they won't. We've nothing to hide.

FRIEDA: So rough they are, so violent, your papers on the
floor –

LAWRENCE: It doesn't matter about that. As long as *you're* all
right –

FRIEDA: And this was on the table.

She holds out the envelope. He looks at it.

LAWRENCE: What is it?

FRIEDA: You had better read it.

LAWRENCE: Why?

He takes it, his fingers stumble with it.

Can't open it. My hands are shaking, look.

FRIEDA: I read it. I read it already.

Beat. They look steadily at each other.

LAWRENCE: How long do they give us?

FRIEDA: Three days. Three days only to get out.

LAWRENCE: Of Zennor?

FRIEDA: Out of *Cornwall.* We are exiled from the whole entire
county.

LAWRENCE sits down slowly.

And when we arrive in London we are ordered to report
directly to the police station in Hampstead. Think, the
shame of it, Lorenzo! To be hounded out of Cornwall and
report to the police like common criminals when we have
done nothing wrong!

LAWRENCE: (*Quietly.*) I wanted to see the winter through.
Everything I've planted. My winter-flowering irises. Red
cabbages and kale.

FRIEDA: Where is your famous English justice system now? How can they call this just, to hound us out for nothing? How can they expect us to pack up everything we have and find a place to live in just three days? It isn't fair, it is not possible, how can we? How can we manage it, Lorenzo? How?

Beat. With a tremendous effort, LAWRENCE strives to reassemble himself.

LAWRENCE: Well, it oughtn't be too hard to find a place in London for a bit.

FRIEDA: A place in London where? For nothing? We have got no *money*, we have nothing!

LAWRENCE: Someone's bound to take us in.

FRIEDA: But you said the London people are the enemy! You said you'd die before you went back there again!

LAWRENCE: Did I say that? Well, things change. The war's changed things. Changed people. It might be good to see a few of the old faces.

FRIEDA: What faces? Who?

LAWRENCE: We could stay with Brett or Dollie Radford for a bit, or Ottoline. It wouldn't be for long. Only a week or two, while we've a chance to think. And then we'll make a plan.

FRIEDA: What sort of plan?

LAWRENCE: (*With a sudden warm enthusiasm.*) You know, it's a queer thing, Frieda, but lately I've found myself thinking about Italy again.

FRIEDA: Italy.

LAWRENCE: Yes. Think how happy we were in Lerici.

FRIEDA: But –

LAWRENCE: And I've been thinking, just imagine – if we could get a group of friends to Italy. I mean, real friends, true friends we can really trust, like William Henry. And set up some sort of community – perhaps a farm –

FRIEDA: Oh no, this cannot be. This is a madness.

LAWRENCE: Look, we chose the wrong people, that's all. It doesn't mean the whole idea should fail. But next time it ought to be in a sunny place, a really sunny place where the land embraces one – where the very climate insists that one must grow and flourish. And where the local people are good folk, simple, rural types, but kindly people who don't judge or question or suspect. Besides, England's no use now, England's done for. We must look abroad now, to a new world, if we're to survive. America, or Italy.

FRIEDA: America?

LAWRENCE: Yes, Florida, or Mexico. Or Italy.

Beat. She looks utterly spent. He pulls her to her feet, covers her in kisses.

My darling, my poor darling, how tired and sad you look! Don't be sad, my love! I'm not. We will come through, you know! We have thousands of lifetimes, Frieda, like the phoenix.

FRIEDA: No, Lorenzo, not the phoenix, I am warning you –

But she is smiling.

LAWRENCE: There, that's my beauty! That's my love! See, like the phoenix – yes, just listen – like the phoenix we've got to submit to it – we've got to be consumed by the mortifying flames, if we're to be reborn, and healed, and live again.

FRIEDA: But I don't want to be consumed by the mortifying flames, Lorenzo. I have had enough of the mortifying flames.

LAWRENCE: But that's just it, my angel, that's the miracle!

FRIEDA: What is?

LAWRENCE's face is now alight. He speaks with a wondering sort of joy.

LAWRENCE: Because every time, over and over, I ask myself: how will we survive this? How will we come through this? Where will we ever find the strength and courage that we need to start again? To start again with *hope*?

Beat.

And then – and then somehow we do.

She looks at him for a long moment.

FRIEDA: Whereabouts in Mexico?

They smile at each other.

Play ends.